ISLE OF HOPE

Michael Hawkes and
Susan Hawkes

with **Stephen Wunderli**

Published by Central Park South Publishing 2022
www.centralparksouthpublishing.com

Copyright © Michael Hawkes and Susan Hawkes, 2022

Typesetting and e-book formatting services by Victor Marcos

ISBN:
978-1-956452-32-7 (pbk)
978-1-956452-33-4 (hbk)
978-1-956452-34-1 (ebk)

I dedicate this book to my best friend,
my eternal partner and wife **Susan**.

We have spent many years searching, laughing and even
shedding tears on this journey. In the end however, we have
found together great joys and unimaginable happiness.

Sharing this journey with you has been
a blessing beyond words.

Grateful.

Michael Hawkes' determination to contribute to a more just Ireland, and a more equal world, inspires us. His efforts to change Irish culture and information laws, by joining in the work of the Clann Project, have been immense. Only by listening to those who have lived forced family separation and childhood abuse can we begin to learn how to prevent such human rights tragedies in future.

— Claire McGettrick

Adoption Rights Alliance co-founder and Clann Project co-director;

—Maeve O'Rourke

Assistant Professor at the Irish Centre for Human Rights, University of Galway, and Clann Project co-director, www.clannproject.org

"Isle of Hope is a heartbreaking read about a dark side of Irish history. Michael Hawkes is a very brave man for sharing his poignant story, which is recommended reading for anybody who wants to better understand what was rotten in the state of Ireland during this period of its infancy as a Republic."

— Jason O'Toole

Best-selling Author and International Journalist

CONTENTS

FOREWORD

I have been following Michael's inspiring story since my father first told me of it years ago. Having now watched Michael's fascinating journey unfold, I have been witness to his resilience and fortitude in sharing this story.

Entangled in a world of government and church collusion to traffic children from Ireland to the United States, Michael shares his harrowing story. He has traveled from separation, loss, abuse, and abandonment to finding hope with family, faith, and heritage.

It has been Operation Underground Railroad's philosophy to recognize that sexual abuse is damaging to individuals and to a society. Sexual Abuse is criminal conduct that cannot be tolerated. Victims must be provided safety and must be treated with dignity and respect. Our goal has been to constantly encourage and advance the empowerment of these victims.

Isle of Hope is an inspiring memoir with a cautionary message to those entrusted with the care and protection of children. Be vigilant.

—Tim Ballard, *Founder and CEO*
Operation Underground Railroad

PROLOGUE

My first memory is not of being guided by gentle hands, or the eyes of my mother as many seem to be able to recall. I was running across a broad lawn in a temporary starched outfit. The stiff shoes were too tight because they too, were not my own. A dark cloud was following me—the flowing black robes of Reverend Mother Josepha. I was making my first attempt at running away to where I did not know. It didn't last long. I felt a sting on the back of my legs that downed me immediately. Howling, I was collected into her arms and brought to a picturesque place to sit astride the dark nun. She bribed me with a piece of candy to stop my tears.

My sister stood frozen on the other side of the draped figure we had come to fear. We were ordered to look at the camera. Sister Josepha tucked the Rosary into her belt having whipped her chattel into submission. She gripped my wrist so tightly I could not open my hand. The camera clicked. My sister and I in our white, borrowed clothes stood out against the black-robed and hooded nun. Satisfied with the marketing photo, she handed us off to another nun who exhorted us to not dirty the white clothes. We changed into our well-worn orphan uniforms. I rubbed at the bead-shaped welts on my leg.

We didn't know then that we were being marketed to rich Americans who didn't qualify for babies through the normal vetting process. We could fetch a high price if the right channels were tapped.

A few miles away, in Armagh, Cardinal McIntyre was being attended to by his secretary, Monsignor Hawkes in preparation for his appearance at Patrician Year celebrations, the 1500-year anniversary of the death of St. Patrick. The dutiful Monsignor was straightening the black simar of the Cardinal, a ceremonial robe with cape that hung from the shoulders to the tops of the feet. The cardinal's waist was wrapped in a scarlet sash; red to represent the blood he was willing to spill for his faith. The Monsignor would check the creases and silk buttons, and brush flecking from the shoulders to ensure only perfection emanated from his eminence.

Monsignor Hawkes was a powerful man in Hollywood; impeccably dressed and often wearing a gold watch. He was the priest to celebrities. His pious business tactics would build the richest diocese in the United States. His accompanying of the Cardinal to Ireland was a sign of his rise in influence. The Cardinal and his procession moved down the cobbled street among stone buildings hundreds of years old. Young Altar Boys led the way carrying brass thuribles of incense and robed in such a way that only their innocent faces were visible. The pomp and ceremony bore little resemblance to Jesus riding into Jerusalem on a humble beast of servitude.

Another mission awaited Monsignor Hawkes. He was to visit a St. Patrick's Guild orphanage. Here he would choose a blessed orphan to be adopted out to America. He had done it for Hollywood elites, he would now do it to elevate his brother's status in Los Angeles. It had to be a boy—Hawkes' brother only had twin daughters. A boy who would become a priest is a free ticket for his parents into Heaven. And a boy could be trained. Hawkes would later be known by his altar boys as "The Priest in Silk Boxers." With the stroke of his pen, he could look the Saint, save his brother, and stock the rectory with another innocent dependent.

We delivered our well-rehearsed greetings to Monsignor Hawkes, we offspring of fallen women with little use but to satiate priests and even nuns who punished children for the sins of their mothers. My sister and I stepped forward. Twins. No connection or knowledge of our mother, wholly dependent on the church for our wellbeing. Perfect. Our staged photos were sent to Bill, Monsignor Benjamin Hawkes' brother. Bill would accept this double offering without reservation.

Five years later I sat on my uncle's lap. He came often to visit his brother. He wore silk stockings, a well-tailored suit and the priest's collar. He treated us to fanciful stories of his travels. He flew on the Concorde to Paris; met with diplomats and movie stars. He famously told other priests "The rich have souls that need saving too." He pulled me tight as he spoke to my adoptive sisters sitting on the floor at his feet; entranced, even infatuated. His hand rested casually on my thigh, sometimes thrumming the inside of my leg intimately close to my crotch as he animated the stories with his other hand. Little did I know I was being groomed.

CHAPTER

One

It's a mysterious thing to see your life unfold backwards, bit by bit as if gathering debris after a cyclone. Yet that is what I have done. With the help of long-lost, yet rediscovered relatives, musty drawers of secretly kept letters and diaries, hidden religious records, reclaimed legal documents, and locked up memories delivered with eruptive emotions at that sacred Irish institution, the pub.

But here I am. And here is the story of a lost Irish baby sold off to Dante himself for a good laugh if it weren't true. I was born in1958. My mother lived in a working-class section of Dublin, around the corner from St. Kevin's Catholic church.

My mother was beaten so severely by her husband James that she ran away as soon as she could walk out of the hospital. They hadn't been married even a year yet. My mother was pregnant. James was a broken man from the Second World War and breaking her seemed to be his only relief. It was a regular occurrence, but the bruises turned into injuries requiring hospitalization,

A Catholic marriage was forever in those days, and sins befell the woman who left. Betty stayed as long as she could, trying to understand her husband's demons. But hope became desperation and Betty chose servitude over death, most likely so she could protect her yet-to-be-born daughter Eilish. Betty fled to her widowed mother's boarding home. She never heard from her husband again. He was buried in the veteran's cemetery. A war hero of record. Nothing more. That is all I know of him. Nothing I've found illuminates their short time together.

Betty began listing herself as a widow on documents. The Church would take care of her the same way they took care of her widowed mother, allowing her to attend Mass if she also helped clean the chapel. Grace for single women was earned in those days.

With her newfound status, Betty was employable at the lowest levels. She worked at the Olympic Ballroom in Dublin, serving tea and libations on weekends while helping her mother with the boarding house, caring for Eilish, and earning her pew in the Church.

Eilish required almost constant attention and tutoring. She was born with challenges and consequently there was no place for her at the Catholic run school, so Betty took care of her during the day and worked weekend nights. The small house afforded one room for Betty and Eilish, another room for her sister Joan, one for mother, and two rooms in the basement for boarders who were mostly university students. There was no privacy. Betty cleaned up after the students, did their laundry, helped prepare meals and maintained a tense relationship with her mother. The work was hard, but at least there was no abuse in the evenings.

Betty escaped to the Olympic Ballroom on the weekends, happy to be alone, even though it meant hours on her feet bussing tables, serving drinks, and washing dishes. And there was music: A live orchestra and people dancing. Eilish was safe at home, asleep. Betty was alive under the hot lights that made the orchestra and dancers sweat. Some of the men smelled of goose grease as it dripped from their slicked back hair onto their faces.

For six years Betty crisscrossed the wooden floor in front of the orchestra, serving young couples who were free to sway to songs that promised a man "was the answer to everything," that "you're nobody until somebody loves you." Betty often caught herself humming these tunes on her way to Mass the next morning where young women would be admonished to prepare for the sacred responsibility of marriage that espoused restraint, prayer, and purity. It was, after all, the woman's responsibility to keep men pure.

But on Saturday nights, she watched young women come into the cloakroom remove their scarves and backcomb their hair. They glossed their lips with fiery red lipstick. It was a sensual transformation as these women arrived bundled up for a night out with friends, so they told their parents, and reddened their cheeks by wetting their fingers and rubbing them on a copy of the Messenger, a religious magazine of the day that was heavy on scarlet ink. They were delighted with the color. Freed from the constraints of gray colors and expectations, they were more than happy to swing into the arms of eager men.

Men wore dark suits and greased their hair back. They trolled the dance floor and picked coy young women who pretended to be modest if their skirts rose too high on a twirl designed for just such an effect. It was a delicate

balance to walk between good Catholic girl and still be
enticing enough to find Mr. Wonderful. The role model
was the Virgin Mary, but reading the prayer book about
sexual taboos aroused young women who longed to shift
(make out) and experience the sexual pleasure forbidden
until marriage

Having been married, Betty understood the longing
of virgin girls. She was 34 years old and not trying to
catch a man. Her experience kept her closed to princess
daydreams yet amused at the young women who came
from the countryside with prayer books in their handbags
and romance on their minds.

Betty had Eilish to take care of, and her mother.
Nobody on the dance floor interested her. But there was a
handsome fellow with a dashing moustache, a saxophone
player in the orchestra. He was mature, married, and safe
to talk to. He stayed late while Betty cleaned up just to
chat with her. He made her smile. He was kind and mature.
It seemed the perfect relationship for Betty: Nonsexual,
non-committal—a friendship with a man who made her
happy just by talking to her.

My mother, Betty was attractive. She had pleasant
features that softened at the cheeks. Her build was slight,
and she carried herself with grace even under the weight
of her life. She missed out on her Mr. Wonderful, but she
accepted where she was.

The Saxophone player's name was Patrick, like half
the men in Ireland. He lived in Dublin but only on the
weekends. He had a good job at Vauxhall in London where
he stayed in a small flat Monday through Friday. He'd
take the Ferry home to his family and play the Olympic
on Saturday nights. He had two boys he adored but Betty

sensed there was some distance between Patrick and his wife although he never talked about the relationship. He was a gentleman.

For two years Betty and Patrick enjoyed each other's company. The Olympic was a hot scene in those days. The women with religiously red cheeks came and went. Betty soaped the lipstick off the glasses. Patrick's orchestra played the most popular tunes. The wooden floor held up under thousands of beating footsteps accompanied by anxious hearts. Betty and Patrick watched it all. The one-night love affairs, the couples that left together and never came back. The singles that never left. And then, it was their turn.

Somewhere their intimate conversations became a trusting physical relationship. It wasn't perfect, it had its share of guilt, but it was a relationship they both wanted, and I honestly believe they were in love. It would be two more years before Betty would wake up one morning feeling sick to her stomach. She called Patrick and he vowed to take care of her, to do the right thing. When so many men had mistresses on the side and tossed them away when they became pregnant, Patrick never thought of Betty as a side girl. He loved her. But the situation was untenable. They both knew it, and like all tragic love stories, they made the best of it before it would end.

Betty sat in Catholic Mass with me, curled up tight as sin in her belly. She knew the weight of condemnation. Priests Like Father McCann standing at the altar in front of her often gave fiery sermons on the evils of premarital sex and the eternal damnation of unmarried pregnant girls. Fingers wagged and tongues clicked at the girls with swollen bellies.

The hypocrisy is that priests who impregnated women themselves were never held accountable—a scandal that still lives in the shadows; the most famous being Father Michael Cleary who in the 1980s got his housekeeper pregnant, twice. The story serves as a portrait of the double standard of the time. Condemnation was slow because other priests were hiding in similar closets. There was hardly a person in Catholic Ireland that didn't have a family member pregnant out of wedlock or fathered an illegitimate child—sometimes both! Yet it was only the fallen women who were considered grave sinners and their children little better, but never the father in the two to tango. In many ways, it was very much a case of love the sin and hate the sinners. Men were often seen as poor victims of the seduction of evil women.

Betty had to leave before being discovered. In her thirties she knew full well what happened to young girls who got pregnant. They were not only ostracized by family and congregation, but also lost any opportunity to work, rent a flat, or even educate their children.

Ireland's Catholic-run orphanages and abuse ridden industrial homes were teeming with unfortunate children either born out of wedlock or snatched from parents deemed unfit to raise them. These frightened women were sent away, perhaps to a mother and baby home, perhaps to a Magdalene laundry, which were glorified prisons for fallen women. They were often forbidden to talk, assigned backbreaking work in the laundry, and beaten for minor infractions.

To avoid a similar fate, Betty would have to create a few lies, disappear for a time—many pregnant women ended up in England—and returned alone as if nothing happened. Common in Ireland at the time were Nuns at train stations patrolling the platforms for young pregnant girls. The girls would be offered help and then quickly swept up and essentially kidnapped and sent to these maternity homes. My mother would have known of these nun dragnets. She would have heard the stories, possibly even knowing of girls from her neighborhood who disappeared. She trusted no one, except Patrick.

She would have to give up the baby on her own, mention the act to no one, return to her life and carry on without Patrick. But what other options did she have? In the new Irish state, undergirded by the power and influence of the Irish Catholic Church, women were defined as mothers and their only valuable contribution to the state was domesticity. Unmarried she had little prospects. Pregnant, she had two options: Secretly give the child up for adoption, or, have an abortion.

Abortions were back-alley affairs then. Illegal. And the famous case of abortionist Mamie Cadden had been in all the papers. Cadden brazenly defied the church and the government by performing abortions. But one of her patients had died and Mamie was on trial for murder. The trial in 1956 became a national spectacle, and a cautionary tale, one that certainly was talked about among women and their daughters. With the sensationalism of the trial only two years prior, it would be hard for my mother to even consider abortion. More importantly, she told her cousin Maura: "I wanted my baby to have a life, a life beyond what could be found with me."

In a few years I would escape from the Isle of Hope, the name I've christened Ireland, borrowed from an Irish song by Brendan Graham: Isle of Hope, Isle of Tears.

Graham's Isle of hope is Ellis Island, in America; the entry point for so many destitute families fleeing famine and British oppression. Ireland in the lyrics is the Isle of hunger and pain left behind. For me, it is the opposite. America was my land of tears. Ireland became my Isle of hope. But to Betty, hope lay somewhere beyond the shores. She would first have to smuggle me to London where I had a fighting chance of being adopted out to a fine family. Her impoverished life would not allow for her to raise another child. She would pretend to be married. Thus, the child was not the spawn of a fallen woman and would enter the world with a little bit of an advantage over the children of single pregnant women who were sentenced to the Magdalene Laundry. There's a good chance my mother would not have survived the Magdalene Laundry. Mine was a high-risk pregnancy with my mother considered advanced maternal age at 36.

Mortality rates for pregnant women in Catholic "charitable institutions" were considerably higher than would be expected, higher than the national average in Ireland. One such home Betty could have ended up in was the Sisters of Our Lady of Charity, who sold off some of their property in Dublin in 1992. The remains of 155 mothers were discovered buried on the grounds in unmarked graves. There but for the grace of God goes my mother.

My mother did not return to church until I was gone, and her secret and sorrow were buried soul deep. Somehow, she remained a faithful Catholic until her death.

CHAPTER

Two

On the night my mother fled for England she left a note telling her mother that she was going to seek work, and that she loved her. She kissed her sleeping daughter Eilish on the forehead and headed out into the freezing January rain. It was 3:30 in the morning. My mother left the note on the fireplace mantle, wrapped her thin coat and scarf around her as tightly as she could and slipped out of the house to give me away. I think about her moving toward the docks, her slight build no match for the cold. She was desperate to move unnoticed onto the ferry to Holyhead, Wales into the unknown. She didn't want to see any familiar faces and be asked awkward questions. Her family would hopefully believe her note—that she was leaving for a few months to work at the biscuit factory where some of her friends had worked over the years.

The Catholic Church pressured unwed mothers into giving up their children to be adopted out "to more deserving families," as the nuns would put it. This was at its heights from 1950-1980s. Babies were often yanked out of the arms of their devastated mothers and told, "It's for the child's best good."

A crash of depression awaited these unwed girls. Many never recovered. Some fell, into abusive relationships, others into prostitution; while drug and alcohol addiction, along with all other forms of hell were prevalent.

In the stiff breeze that misted the ferry with a penetrating cold, uncertainty fraught with stories of abortionists and the fate of unwed mothers and their babies must have cut into her like the icy gusts. Betty stood nervously on the dock and watched as the ferrymen of the British and Irish Steam Packet Company, known as the B&I line, prepared for the early morning sail to Holyhead. Here were men with jobs and families. Their hands thick and rough from a life of work outdoors, their faces weathered beyond their years. But they were working, and bringing home paychecks, not coins from tips that Betty kept in a milk bottle. Her own father had died when she was incredibly young. It seemed like she was pressing against the storms her whole life. Her head dropped against the wind.

As she waited to board, Betty's fatigued mind must have drifted to thoughts of Patrick Ryan. She had known him for more than 4 years. Patrick was thirteen years older than her, he was a handsome Dubliner, tall and with a thick mop of hair combed neatly back. She remembered dancing with him the first time, saying to herself: "Has it really been ten years since I danced with anyone at this hall?" They would stay up most of the night, often dancing alone behind the building until the sky lightened into gray just before the sun came up. Betty had Eilish to worry about. I think now about how strong a woman my mother was. Like Cinderella, she hurried home to her drudgery and waited for the next weekend. She had devoted the last nine years of her life to her little girl and gave herself one evening a week to be happy. She longed for the kind of man that could match her strength of character yet let her finally be vulnerable. She found him in Patrick, at the wrong time.

In Betty, Patrick found a strong soul with a heart that had never fully been set free to express affection. He let her talk about the lighter things in life to distract her from the weight she carried. Gradually, she opened up and could trust him. Betty rubbed tears that had escaped from her tired eyes as she walked through the night. "How could I have let this get so out of control?" she thought.

As she waited for the ferry departure on that dreary, early winter morning, she also rehearsed how she had discovered she was pregnant, how she approached Patrick one evening after their work at the Olympic. She was horrified to tell him, but knew he was her only confidante and would not leave her without helping. She had a rough go of hiding her nausea during the months and her slender body struggled to hide a growing abdomen. She lived daily with the angst of being discovered. And now she was about to do the unthinkable. I see my mother's life as years-worth of hardship interrupted by a fleeting period of happiness with Patrick. I'm grateful to him.

The ferry horn blew its final warning, startling Betty from her thoughts. She hurried herself, gathering her small bag. With all the emotional strength she had, my mother rushed across the walkway into the economy pedestrian cabin. She found a seat in the back corner, scanning the cabin for any familiar faces. Thankfully, she didn't see anybody she knew, and she quickly slouched into her seat, pulled the scarf tightly around her face and readied herself for the rough eight-hour sea journey to Holyhead, to a place unknown.

I rode that ferry on one of my trips later in age to honor my mother's journey. I left from the same dock in Dublin. There was no rain that day, only the ever-present dampness that foretells a storm. My wife and I boarded the ferry and found our seats. Here we were on a much faster, more comfortable passenger ferry. Our trip was one of discovery and ease. I thought of my mother's arduous ferry experiences and her fear of being discovered. All her plans were dependent on the success of this trip.

London would be the farthest Betty had ever travelled from home. She would have to find the right train to London after arriving in Holyhead. She must avoid inquiring nuns. Patrick would meet her and make sure she had a flat until the baby arrived. He would meet her at Euston in London and escort her. A noble thing in those days, but she still must've had her doubts.

I think Patrick did what he could for my mother. I often think if times were different, they may have ended up together. Those kinds of improprieties cost people their families, careers, and station in the oppressed social structure of that era.

Betty watched the approaching port of Holyhead from the ferry's window. She had slept a few hours of the eight-hour sea voyage, waking to eat a cheap packed lunch. The second half of the ferry trip had seen rough seas. The ferry accommodated people and their vehicles, and farm animals. The smell from animals must have surely been overpowering to Betty's exaggerated sense of smell and nausea developed in pregnancy. The only way to keep your lunch down is by breathing in the fresh marine air on the deck just outside the cabins.

As soon as the ferry docked, she was eager to disembark and find the train station. She kept her hands wrapped in her scarf to hide a ringless finger. So much of this I surmise because Betty recounted much of the story to her cousin Maura who had kept it for 56 years.

The ferry, scheduled to arrive at 3pm, docked on time. Betty walked off the ferry and followed the signs to the train station. She found a kind and helpful man at the ticket counter who helped put her on a train to Euston. No doubt he would have been dismissive if he knew she was single and pregnant. She anxiously waited for her train on the platform, asking several people if they knew if the platform was the correct one to Euston. Once on the train, she relaxed a bit.

During the nearly four-hour train trip, Betty reflected on how she had always dreamed of visiting London. It was an angst-ridden contradiction to be living a dream and a nightmare at the same time. But Betty vowed to make the experience as positive as possible. Armed with her newfound confidence from navigating the nighttime journey from Dublin to the Ferry to Holyhead and the train to Euston, she pondered what she might do in London during the months left until the birth.

The train porter announced the approaching Euston station. Betty was anxious about finding Patrick after dark but had no doubt he would be at the station. As the ferry had arrived on time, she had caught the train he recommended from the schedule. Despite their indiscretions, she knew Patrick to be responsible, as he had supported her as much as he was able, in the last four months after learning of her pregnancy. He would be there; she knew it and knew him.

Betty stepped off the train, onto the platform and walked out to the Euston terminal. Patrick was standing just outside the turnstile. He greeted her warmly but distantly. Patrick was troubled deeply at what had to be done. It would be a secret he would take to his grave. They had decided, despite their love for each other that after this ordeal was over, they would go their separate ways; he back to his wife and sons; Betty back to Dublin and her daughter and mother. The pregnancy had shocked them both back into the reality of their complicated lives.

Patrick took Betty's small bag and led her out to the busy street. They waited at a bus stop in silence, await which must have been shrouded in anxiety, before travelling the short distance to the small flat he had rented in London's East End.

CHAPTER

Three

*B*etty and Patrick crossed the threshold of the door to the London flat, into a life of pretend. Patrick said with regret, as they entered the small living space, "It isn't Buckingham Palace, but it's safe and clean."

Patrick was providing for his wife and sons back in Dublin, and maintained a flat in Luton, adjacent to the automobile factory where he was employed, approximately 30 kilometers northeast from the East End. He was now financially responsible for this third abode. The secrets he kept to protect my mother is admirable. How he was able to add this flat to his monthly expenses and keep it a secret is difficult to fathom. Perhaps he paid for it with his gig money from the Olympic. I could not find out.

The flat itself was cramped; it had a tiny kitchen with a small metal table and two chairs. Adjacent to the table were two high back chairs and a lamp table in a sitting area: all surprisingly clean for the noticeable age of the furnishings. The one bedroom had hardly room for the single metal bed frame with a mattress that was flat, most likely horsehair, and hard. The toilet and bath were shared spaces down the hall, which would have filled those daily trips to the loo with trepidation. A strange building. Judging eyes. A growing belly.

It was a bustling city's version of *The Valley of the Squinting Windows,* that story about neighbors who won't mind their business and wish everybody to fail. *"Who is this pregnant woman living alone who doesn't go out much?"* There must have been gossip, the kind purposely whispered loud enough for her to hear.

Patrick told her, "I made some discrete enquiries and located the closest Crusade of Rescue office, very near here." Betty was relieved and planned to visit in the morning, hoping to be referred to a clinic. She was anxious to determine if the baby was doing well and to confirm her due date.

The next morning, Betty was waiting on the steps as the Catholic Children's Society Crusade of Rescue East End offices opened. It was a dreary morning, gray air; the sidewalks crossed with that class of people whose hands are often calloused. She visited with the Society nuns, stating her need for prenatal care. She was one in a room full of similar women, exiles from belligerent boyfriends, castoffs from pious families, discarded mistresses, and wives too poor to seek services somewhere else. The Society was their only hope, and the world-weary nuns the gatekeepers. The stark room, sparsely furnished, mismatched chairs filled with trembling mothers-to-be, the lack of emotion struck her. "Is there not a God for us?" she wondered.

Betty was checked in and referred to a midwifery clinic as if she were filing for the dole. After leaving the Society she walked the half-kilometer to the address and found herself standing in front of a building adjacent to a

Church of England. A temporary sign had been placed at the front doors: Midwifery Clinic Every Thursday. Here was a small bit of hope. At least she would have help delivering the baby.

Betty approached the clinic, signed in at the front makeshift reception area, just inside the multipurpose hall, and took a seat, as directed by the receptionist. My mother joined several dozen women, most noticeably pregnant, sitting in folding chairs, some with newborn infants in their arms, others with toddlers at their feet. Two-thirds of the large space was set up with temporary partitions, separating obstetrical examination gurneys. The groans and the conversations during those examinations were clearly heard throughout the room. Self-dignity was sacrificed. Betty began the paperwork she had been given on a clipboard.

An hour and a half later, she heard a voice calling from the examination area, "Mrs. Elizabeth Mancell"?

Betty used her married name. She and Patrick would pretend to be married. Nurse Williams introduced herself and directed Betty into one of the partitioned examination cubicles. Betty lied to Nurse Williams as she explained her situation. "My husband and I have just moved here from Cork for his work. I wish to continue my care and deliver our baby here. This is my second pregnancy, but it's been over eight years since our daughter's birth."

Nurse Williams asked some questions about Betty's family medical history and financial situation. Betty explained that they had little money for medical bills and provided a written statement of their income specifics that established their need for charitable care. Betty's vital signs were taken; she was relieved that all seemed normal.

Nurse Williams helped Betty to lie on the exam table and explained that, based on the last menstrual period reported; a due date of June 7th would be likely.

Nurse Williams began examining Betty's abdomen and said, "I estimate you to be further along than you had thought. Are you certain you could not have conceived a month earlier?"

Betty, very confused, stated, "No, prior to that month, I … my husband works abroad, and we had not been intimate for over three months."

Nurse Williams began the examination. "That should help determine a more accurate due date. Because it has been so long, nine years, since you delivered a baby, this labor and delivery will likely be nearly as long as the first."

The midwife paused as she felt Betty's abdomen for fetal position and size, "I stand corrected, this pregnancy will be altogether different. You, my dear Mrs. Mancell, are carrying twins!"

Betty felt the blood drain from her face. She tried to pass off her tears as ones of joy, but she thought to herself, 'Two babies to love, two babies to lose." This pain and loss multiplied would nearly break her heart.

In Britain alone, religious institutions ran over 150 mother and baby homes, the sort of birthing centers with two exits, one for the empty-handed mother and the other for the child to be adopted out to more worthy parents. An estimated 16,000 babies were adopted out through these mother baby homes run by the Catholic Church, the Church of England, and the Salvation Army in the 50s, 60s. The rushed process in the name of providing more godly homes circumvented even the most common-sense vetting procedures. Betty knew she had to give up her babies. What she didn't know was the system of adopting them out was designed to protect the appearances of the Catholic Church as the paternal caretaker. The Church knew best and cut the bonds between mother and child. Fallen women were ostracized; babies were farmed out to Catholic families. The Church was judge and executor.

My sister and I would soon be moved like goods in a factory line.

A young mother identified only as Margaret, who was sent to a Salvation Army maternity home in Leeds, told the Guardian in 2016: "I'd like people to know that you didn't give your babies away. They were taken from you, and you didn't have a choice." She recalled a member of staff coming to collect her baby: "And she [said], 'Don't be silly, you're doing what's best,' and took him from my arms and went, and you're just left in that room crying and not one person came to you. She didn't come back to me after she'd taken the baby." And so, it was for thousands of young, single mothers in the delirium of post delivery, were separated from their own flesh and blood.

In addition to seeing the midwives at the clinic monthly, Betty was also scheduled for regular visits with an obstetrician at the local community hospital. Betty's advanced maternal age, coupled with the twin pregnancy and continued unstable positions of the babies, made her a high-risk patient who required increased monitoring. Childbirth in 1950's England was a cold affair. My mother could look forward to giving birth alone, with no anesthesia, no comfort. It would be an institutional exercise. Her status as married, albeit fabricated, did afford her less condemnation, but poverty was a sin too, and she paid for it with every visit.

As she waited for a second midwife appointment in February 1958, Betty was in conversation with a fellow Irish woman named Margaret, who was also seeking care for a pregnancy. Margaret was a woman in her late thirties as well, having her sixth baby. Margaret and Betty were commenting about the number of Irish men forced to find work abroad and live either alone in poor conditions or, if lucky, with their families in England.

Margaret stated, "It explains why there are so many of us from Ireland delivering our babies in London. Those numbers don't account for all the unmarried girls coming here to deliver to hide their pregnancies or to get rid of them. I heard the receptionists complaining about the large numbers—thousands per year apparently—of Irish fallen women they see in the clinics!"

The receptionists said they were called PFI—Pregnant from Ireland! "Dirty little Irish babies" was often heard muttered by English women at the clinic as well as nuns. The clinic could just as well have been an asylum, with it's rusty iron beds, hand-me-down examination tables, worn tiles and the lack of sunlight. But it was a far cry better than the facilities that housed fallen women disowned by their families before they delivered. Many ended up at Mother Baby homes, like the one at Tuam.

In 1975, Mary Moriarty was living in the subsidized housing built on the property where the Mother and Baby home in Tuam had been. It was close to Halloween and a neighbor had told her that a boy was running about scaring children with a skull on a stick. Mary went to investigate.

Examining the skull, Mary told the boy it was not plastic, but real, the skull of a small child. She ordered the boy to put the skull back where he found it and followed him to the location. The boy led Mary through the rubble and weeds on the edge of the Mother and Baby home that had been run by the Catholic Church, more specifically the order Bon Secours Sisters. As she crossed the soft ground, suddenly the earth beneath her feet gave way and Mary fell into some kind of tunnel or cave. There was just enough light to illuminate her surroundings. Stacked neatly like flour packets in a cellar were little bundles the size of a loaf of bread wrapped tightly in gray cloth. Climbing out of the catacomb, Mary was horrified. She contacted an older woman in the neighborhood who used to work at the home. "Ah, yeah," the woman said, peering into the collapsed hole. "That's where the little babies are."

The discovery at Tuam rocked all of Ireland. A society so tightly managed by the morality of the Catholic Church, and so entangled in the acts of government pertaining to citizens and their own children cut to the heart of what it meant to be Irish. After years of investigating, 796 bodies were discovered in chambers of the septic system connected to the Mother and Baby home in Tuam. At first there was denial, saying the skeletal remains were from the famine. But death records were uncovered of the babies at the home. None of which received a proper burial.

His voice trembling with emotion, the Prime Minister Enda Kenny addressed the Irish legislature on what he called the chamber of horrors at Tuam. "We dug deep and we dug deeper still," he said. "To bury our compassion, to bury our mercy, to bury our humanity itself."

What did the children die of? Mistreatment. In 1947, a government health inspector filed a report describing the conditions of infants in the nursery: "a miserable emaciated child…delicate…occasional fits…emaciated and delicate...fragile abscess on hip...not thriving wizened limbs emaciated...pot-bellied emaciated...a very poor baby..." 52 babies died that year. Unnoticed babies, children of the devil consigned with their fallen mothers to a life of suffering for their sins.

In 2017, after the news broke on live television, the Bon Secours Sisters hired a public relations agency to discredit the find. But it was too late.

Such was the Ireland I was born into, with a scant chance of making it.

Betty and Patrick continued to pose as Mr. and Mrs. Patrick Mancell with the clinic and their landlord. However, Betty was desperate for help. She had to be candid with the nuns at East End offices of the Catholic Children's Society Crusade of Rescue. She was desperate for their help in arranging for the babies' placement after they were born.

Betty sat at her little kitchen table in the flat and wrote a painfully honest letter to the Sister in charge telling her, "I am ashamed to have been keeping time with a married man and had found myself pregnant with twins." She further wrote, "I was living with my mother at home, and I left home, leaving a letter saying, 'I was going to work.' If she knew the truth, it would kill her, and she would never let me home again, and I do want to see my little girl again."

The letter pains me to read. Knowing Patrick would soon be gone, and that her babies would be adopted, Betty chose to be vulnerable to this nun. It saddens me to read the letter. Her small body could barely carry the weight of the two babies, let alone the uncertainty that waited. I can't imagine the state she must have been in to trust the nun so completely.

Betty's pregnancy progressed. On April 28th, five weeks early, Betty went into labor. As Patrick was at work in Luton that morning, Betty borrowed the phone of the landlord to call the Midwifery clinic number. The midwives arranged to escort Betty to the hospital and got word to Patrick in Luton. Betty made the painful walk from her flat to the clinic, enduring the stares, and shuffling along the uneven sidewalk. From there, she was driven by the midwives to the hospital. Patrick stoically went about his work at the Vauxhall factory spray painting automobile chassis and forcing himself to remain composed.

On arrival that evening, Patrick rushed into the hospital with apprehension and some fear. Here he was at Betty's labor, a woman not his wife. The thought of being discovered must have haunted him during every waking hour. He was informed that Betty was still in labor but progressing nicely. Just after midnight, a nurse approached Patrick in the waiting room. She said, "Congratulations, you have a beautiful little girl born just before midnight; followed by a darling boy, born just after midnight."

A feigned delight followed, one that blanketed Patrick's anxiety. He held Betty's hand and stayed the night at her bedside. Twins, a boy and a girl that could be his to raise under different circumstances.

In the morning, the happy couple separated for the day. Patrick off to work, Betty waving goodbye. Betty nursed the twins and was addressed as Mrs. Mancell. It was a fantasy that would keep her going. But underlying the façade was angst. She sent a desperate letter to the administrating Sister of the Crusade of Rescue, "My babies are born, a girl and a boy, and both perfect, a really good weight too. Please don't let the hospital know. They are making a great fuss of me and I know they would be very disappointed if they knew what I intended to do. Could you write to me without letting the hospital know? I will be here I'm sure for about eight more days. I will not be able to go to Cork, as I will not be well enough. I feel very weak, neither can I afford to keep the babies. I have no hope at all of keeping them with no money. Could you take the babies until I am well enough to work? I certainly can't go home to my mother. I hope to hear from you soon. Please make it urgent. Respectfully, Betty Mancell."

Patrick visited each day, but the pain on his face grew deeper. He held a smile the day we were discharged— Betty and the babies, my sister and me, Michael Anthony. As far as the hospital staff knew, Betty and Patrick were a delighted, somewhat older couple, who just added two darling babies to their family. As much as Betty hoped that she might be able to find work and keep the babies, she had little experience that would lead to a job with which she could support herself and her babies. Even as a married woman in 1950's Ireland, it was nearly impossible to be gainfully employed. Women were expected to be about their domestic duties. Only 30% of the workforce was female.

Working women were perceived as taking jobs away from men and therefore consigned to the service industries. Single mothers were cast-offs, living in the backrooms of washhouses and raising their children in Dickensian shame. Unemployment in Ireland in the 1950s was at a record high. So was emigration. Ireland was in the midst of an economic crisis forcing cuts to food assistance programs. Betty's husband James was not dead and therefore she didn't qualify for a widow's pension, or the meager assistance afforded to children at the time. And she now had three. Had she qualified for a pension, the government assumed that pensioners lived with family and that the pension was meant to augment their living situation, not provide for all the living expenses. Thus, we see why Betty's mother lived below the poverty line and took boarders for income. Betty had no employment options, did not qualify for assistance, and was lucky to have her job bussing tables at the Olympic to earn enough to take care of Eilish.

It's no wonder Betty and Patrick were anxious to find a way to get the babies safely adopted before going their separate ways. Betty wrote again to the Catholic Children's Society Crusade of Rescue's East End Office, asking for assistance in getting the babies adopted in Ireland. The Society again contacted the Child Protection and Rescue Society of Ireland, originally established to keep Catholic children in Catholic institutions and homes, away from Protestant influence. Betty was encouraged to get the babies back to Ireland, in an effort to be more likely to facilitate a Catholic adoption or placement.

My mother's last bit of hope was that her children would grow up in Ireland and that someday she could meet them, tell them her story, release years of love, devotion, and anguish in the reunion. However, the logistics of getting two newborns back to Dublin was proving difficult, even for the two Catholic collaborating societies of rescue.

After being discharged from the hospital, Betty and the babies lived in the small flat with the shared bathroom waiting for accommodation assistance for travel back to Ireland. Her days consisted of feeding, changing, washing diapers, and trying to sleep, which she found quite difficult.

Patrick was stretched between working flat-out Monday through Friday at the Luton factory, going to Dublin twice a month, by train and ferry, to visit his family and continue his weekend work with the Olympic Orchestra. The train journey from Luton to the East End took 45 minutes. Each day he hopped the train after working, visited with Betty in the evening to give her some respite from caring for two newborns alone and traveled back on the last train to Luton, in order to work the next morning. The street where the flat was located was a noisy place, day and night. Betty would fall asleep holding one of the babies, while Patrick held the other, getting a few precious hours of rest.

Reading these details in my mother's letters and loose diary gives me profound respect for Patrick. I can see why my mother loved him. These emotional burdens must have weighed heavily on him. Perhaps it is my own romantic notion of my biological father, but I imagine him playing in the orchestra to unbind his heart from the duress of the life he had fallen into, while trying to do the right thing. Every extra pound he earned at the ballroom was spent on the East End flat. And still, he was stretched thin, financially, and emotionally.

Betty arranged for us to be baptized when we were five weeks old at St. Mary of the Angels Catholic Church, Bayswater, London. This would require Betty and Patrick to be married so they listed Patrick Mancell as the father on the birth certificate, using Betty's married name. This would prove to be a clue to be followed, many years later. Betty couldn't have known how fortuitous it would be to use her married name and Patrick's first name. Call it divine serendipity.

On the baptismal certificates, however, no father was listed. Fabricating Church documents was not something

Patrick or Betty could even contemplate. To deceive the Church was to deceive God. And my mother wanted redemption. In her mind, the only way to see her children again would be by some God-given miracle.

Still at the flat, on July 9th, Betty penned another desperate letter to the rescue society administrator:

> *Could you please do something soon about the adoption of my twins? We are starving. I am not well.*
>
> *I told the midwife in the clinic how I feel, and she said I am not getting enough food to nurse two babies and recover. I am bleeding and not getting enough rest.*
>
> *The babies are a terrible handful, and I will not have the energy to travel. I feel very sick indeed, so could you please try to arrange some place for me here in England? I would be more than grateful. Please do something soon, as if I do get really very ill, they will really have to be taken then.*
>
> *I love the babies. If I could, I would keep them, but I have nothing for them, to keep them with. They will know who I am soon, and it will be harder on me and them if they are not adopted soon. I do hope you understand my position and try to hurry things.*
>
> *Please excuse my awful scribble, as I am in a rush in case the babies wake.*
>
> *Yours respectfully, Betty Mancell.*

Betty received a hand delivered note from the East End rescue society on July 17, when we babies were nearly three months old. The Catholic Protection and Rescue Society of Ireland made arrangements for Betty and babies to travel by train and ferry to Dublin, where we'd all be temporarily housed at the Regina Coeli Hostel, a homeless shelter for mothers and their children. Betty was heartbroken yet encouraged that the struggles to return and get us placed in Ireland were nearly at an end.

Returning to Dublin required Betty to take the B&I route with us. Her cousin Maura's husband was employed as a steward on that B&I ferry route and Betty feared being discovered. But this was the only option. Betty had to fall in with whatever plans were necessary. She also worried that, should she be required to call at the CPRSI offices, on Dublin's South Anne Street, she would be just around the corner from her mother's home on Synge Street. The whole affair began to take on a clandestine feeling that made my mother uneasy.

Betty faced the day she left with great faith. In her weakened state she believed God would deliver her and the babies through the emissaries of the Catholic Church. This faith, in the face of oppressive institutions in God's name astounds me. How could she even believe in the deliverance God would provide when navigating the complexities of religious institutions that alternately degraded and assisted, always with an air of piousness meant to put sinners like Betty in their place and keep them there? Betty had no choice but to rely on the hand that shamed and fed her.

On August 16, 1958, physically and emotionally weak, Betty struggled to get the second-hand pram through the Euston station train doors. My twin sister and I, now nearly four months old, were on our way to Dublin, tightly packed into a pram built for one. Patrick had booked passage on the train and ferry for himself as well and watched from afar to ensure that we three were safe. He did so in secret because it was a route he travelled regularly, which meant many Dubliners may recognize him. He knew he could not make contact on the ferry, only watch helplessly as Betty struggled with the pram. I wonder what he must have thought as he observed poor Betty who was gaunt and a little pale from blood loss.

Betty boarded the ferry with babies in tow and found the same isolated corner as before in which to hide as much as possible. An Irish woman, traveling alone, with a pram carrying two babies, was very conspicuous.

The hours long ferry crossing was arduous, with two hungry babies to soothe and feed. Patrick intentionally sat a few seats back. He couldn't risk helping publicly, but at one point he could no longer resist as his heart pained. He approached Betty when both babies were crying.

"Pardon me madam, may I offer some help? I would be happy to hold a baby for a while," he said loudly for others within earshot to hear.

Betty and Patrick both held back tears as she allowed the pretend stranger to hold and soothe me. He was well-dressed and looked to be a kind soul lending a hand to a struggling mother.

The jolting, rocking ferry pushing through the chop of the sea made it difficult to calm the babies. But with both of us in familiar arms, we quieted. We were gently placed back in the pram. Patrick gently crept back into the shadows to keep an eye from behind a newspaper.

Betty sighed, the gentle rocking of the sea took over and she was about to rest herself when she looked up to see her cousin Eddie approaching her. Eddie was shocked and very confused to see Betty with two babies. And Betty was mortified to see him. A sobbing Betty pleaded, "Eddie you can't tell anyone of the babies!"

Eddie, a young and loving father to his own little family, said convincingly to Betty, "I will hold your secret in confidence, but please let us help you! Please let me tell Maura so that we can both do what we can for you and the babies."

Patrick looked on helplessly. Seeing Betty's distraught reaction, he knew her fears of being seen by her cousin had been realized. For nearly a year, Patrick and Betty had kept the pregnancy and births secret. Patrick was sick with worry now about Eddie discovering the sinful truth. He was desperately struggling with his own grief at losing two children. He hoped that there would be some kind of goodbye when they reached Dublin. But now even that was gone. All that remained was his faith that *his* twins would find good lives in adopted homes.

Eddie discovering us on that rough passage turned out to be a great gift. Maura and Betty were remarkably close. Over the next few weeks, they talked about everything. Each detail I have recounted so far came mostly from long conversations Maura and Betty shared. Maura locked them away; each emotional scene recounted to her and held them for 56 years.

On arrival, Betty allowed Eddie to help her to the Regina Coeli Hostel. She tried to steal a glance at Patrick, but he had disappeared into the foot traffic. They would never see each other again.

The next day, Maura and Eddie arrived to visit Betty and babies. Maura and Betty were the same age and had been very close first cousins. Maura convinced Betty to come to their home during the daytime, though rules required that Betty and the babies return to the hostel in the evenings, to secure their place and to facilitate the eventual relinquishment—their word—for adoption of the babies. I think of that word "relinquishment," so cold as if babies were articles in a lease agreement.

Maura and Eddie were a godsend. This brief period in their care allowed my mother to heal enough to move forward. Eddie's wages were just enough to care for his small family. He and Maura were the parents of a toddler and Maura was eight months pregnant with their second child. Maura had suffered two pregnancy losses and ached thinking of the loss that would be Betty's when she had to give up the babies. Maura and Eddie thought long and hard about whether they could take in the babies as their own, but eventually concluded that they could not feed so many mouths. It was heartbreaking to hear Maura tell me this. She ached right up until the day we met so many years later.

Maura convinced Betty to let Maura's aunt Catherine in on the secret. Catherine was the younger sister of Betty's mother and had always been kind and tender. During the weeks Betty and we were housed at the cramped hostel that offered little privacy. Catherine and Maura—and Eddie, when not on duty on the B&I line—would take us into their home. It gave my mother a glimpse of life as it could be: two parents who love each other. They offered her comfort without judgment.

When the day came to "relinquish" us, Maura and Catherine arrived in the early morning at the hostel.

Catherine had brought strips of clean muslin cloth. Betty was quietly weeping in her room as she nursed each of us one last time. She held her babies close, trembling so uncontrollably that we babies had difficulty eating.

Catherine helped Betty bind her breasts with the muslin strips to help the milk supply dry up. Then Catherine and Maura helped Betty push the pram down the cobbled streets to the Catholic Protection Rescue Society of Ireland on South Anne Street, only a stone's throw from the house in which she herself grew up. Maura, due to deliver her baby any day, cried quietly as she looked on as Catherine and Betty walked the two babies through an imposing red door, the door of relinquishment I stood at some 56 years later.

Betty reluctantly signed those relinquishment papers with a shaking hand, praying for a quick placement and better life than she could provide for her beloved babies. The society had arranged for a court order to be made for the taking of the twins, a formality, Betty was told, that would expedite the placement of the babies. She had given up her babies by legal decree and the finality of it struck deep in her heart.

Leaning heavily on Catherine, Betty exited through the finality of the red door, broken and grief stricken.

Maura was thankful that no one had seen the act, that God had somehow let them pass unnoticed on the streets. Betty wept bitterly until she had no tears left. She visited with Maura one last time, long enough to put her hand to the belly and feel the kicks of the unborn baby. And then numb, and in shock, she began the lonely walk home.

The streets did not seem the same, those narrow streets she had grown up on, had fled to, battered, and broken, to be eyed by pious churchgoers. It was a port to return to, but not a safe harbor. As she walked along, she passed St. Kevin's church where Father McCann was pruning his rose garden. Here is the priest who meted out condemnation and trimmed away thorns and useless stalks. Betty hurried by. She had so many questions, but none could be answered by this priest. She walked around the corner to her mother's home on Synge Street, slipping quietly through the door she had exited over seven long months before.

Betty had missed Eilish's ninth birthday. She held nine-year-old Eilish and rocked her like a baby. She was relieved to be home, to have it completed, yet broken to have just relinquished two other children: broken to her very soul.

CHAPTER

Four

*T*he same day we were relinquished, we, as five-month-old babies, were both sent to Kilkenny. My sister was delivered to St. Joseph's Girls Home; I was delivered to St. Patrick's Boys Home. Intake records documented an incarceration charge of, "not having any home." The log listed the "sentence of detention" as until "April 27, 1974", the day before we would turn 16-years-old. And thus began our lives as "criminals" with a sentence, held on the charge of being unwanted spawn of a fallen woman. The medieval language always strikes me as being barbaric and cruel.

The Catholic Protection and Rescue Society officials required a statement from the father of the children. The solicitor provided this letter: *"Mr. Ryan has told us that he raises no objection to his two children and whose mother is Mrs. Mancell, being adopted and he acknowledges that he is the father of these children."*

This single document, a breadcrumb in a park full of pigeons, led me to my father years later. It would require some Holmesian deduction and a little cajoling on my

wife's part to obtain it. Until then, it sat buried in a stack
of papers at St. Patrick's Guild.

We were wards of the Catholic Church.

The next two and a half years were spent in a long
corridor with baby cribs on either side. I have no memory
of the place, only photographs of the orphanage, the rooms,
the austere nuns posing perfectly in starched white robes.
Even their shoes were spotless. It is a memory constructed
from books, records, and photographs, but no emotion. I
have read accounts of mothers who were allowed to visit
their babies in the months before they were adopted out.
But they are rare, and I had no such experiences.

How my sister and I ended up on an airplane to
America is in itself, I believe, a series of legal sidesteps and
moral deflection. In my research of my history, one could
surmise "Good Catholic" families who didn't pass the
vetting process in America could get babies from Ireland
through the Catholic Church if they made large enough
donations. At the very least this skirts due process, at
worst it amounts to I believe, child trafficking. I will let
the reader decide. But consider two things: an estimated
2,100 Irish babies were adopted out to American families,
some to parents with histories of abuse, and many who had
been rejected by American adoption agencies or policies.
My own adoption papers were signed by the much-feared
John Charles McQuaid, the Archbishop of Dublin. He
posthumously faced a history of sexual abuse allegations
himself and was the subject of a controversial biography,
aided by an unpublished essay by one of his archenemies,
the politician Dr Noel Browne. McQuaid was accused of
attempting to sexually assault a teenage boy in a Dublin pub.
I wonder what else was covered up by the frocks around him.

Before our plane trip, my sister and I were brought back together to Dublin in March 1961. We were placed at St. Patrick's, Blackrock Temple Hill, a holding pen for Irish adoption, run by St. Patrick's Guild, of the Sisters of Charity. It was The Patrician Year: 1961. Celebrations and ceremonies were planned all over the island. This was the celebration of the fifteenth centenary of the death of Saint Patrick, who banished all the snakes out of Ireland. (Unfortunately, that did not include the proverbial ones.)

The Opening Ceremonies occurred on St. Patrick's Day, 1961, during which processions and ceremonies occurred in the city of Armagh. Catholic dignitaries from all over the world were invited. Ireland had not been allowed its own Cardinal at that time, so a foreign Cardinal was invited to preside over the Patrician Year events.

Cardinal McIntyre of the Archdiocese of Los Angeles was invited to preside. He arrived with his entourage from America, including his secretary, Monsignor Benjamin Hawkes. The entourage, in addition to ceremonial duties, toured and inspected Catholic Institutions in Ireland, specifically Patrician institutions. Monsignor Hawkes was given the grand tour expected for a man of the cloth with his stature in the world of St. Patrick's, Black Rock, Temple Hill. He had become priest to the stars in Los Angeles and would later design his own church with soaring, angled ceilings that knifed their way through the sky into Heaven.

Monsignor Hawkes would break from all the pageantry to do something pedestrian, tour Temple Hill. I speculate that he wanted a pious gesture to elevate his status by securing a boy for his brother and sister-in-law back in the U.S. Bill and Helen were devout, yet 46 years old, which was beyond the legal age for adoption in America. They had two older girls.

Any red tape could be overcome and expedited. This was a celebrity priest, who could get what he wanted in the name of God. I was dressed up and paraded in front of Monsignor Hawkes, who had made this trip before finding children for celebrities because they too wanted to cut through the red tape seemingly. When he was told I had a twin sister he called his brother immediately.

A letter from St. Patrick's Guild arrived at the home of Bill and Helen Hawkes in Saratoga, California, dated 10 April 1961. It was little more than a formality since Monsignor Hawkes position would make any vetting unnecessary. The letter read, "Dear Mr. and Mrs. Hawkes, Many Thanks for papers received relative to the adoption of a child from this Agency. We note that the State Department of Public Welfare are in process of preparing a Home Study Report for you, and as soon as we receive it, we shall pass your application on to His Grace, our Archbishop, for his approval."

The archbishop referenced was the aforementioned John Charles McQuaid, the main architect of adoption policy in Ireland and enabler of trafficking it seems, of Irish babies to the United States, and a pedophile himself. McQuaid's directives for allowing adoptions of a Catholic child by a foreign or American family included being recommended by the family parish priest and local diocesan director of Catholic Charities, and the swearing of an affidavit that they would educate the adopted child in Catholic schools and raise the child Catholic.

Unwritten was the pledge of continued generous donations to the Church. *Generous* donations. No further vetting necessary. I'm not even sure any interviews by the State Department of Welfare even took place. What I have learned is, many adoptions were signed only by two priests: one representing the baby, and the other representing the adoptive parents. Wash your hands, repeat.

There was an historical reason why Irish babies were being adopted out to Americans. After the war, US servicemen were stationed in Ireland. Some of them got Irish women pregnant, who were then left with no resources to care for the child. I'd recommend watching six-time Academy Award nominee Jim Sheridan's poignant film about it, *The Secret Scripture*. Shunned by their communities, and with no social safety nets, the Irish government relied on the Catholic Church to take care of these fallen women and their babies, which was seen as a national embarrassment.

Add to that the number of Irish babies already landing in orphanages, it left the Irish government dependent on the Catholic church to sweep it all under the carpet. Up until 1957, for an American to adopt an Irish baby all you had to do was secure a passport for the child, which wasn't really very difficult. Actress Jane Russell went through this dubious process and suddenly the bright lights turned to a system that seemed to be marketing babies like canned goods.

The operation fell to Catholic Relief services headed by Monsignor O'Grady in Ireland. No questions were asked about the possibility of babies being sold on the black market. What if these innocent children ended up homeless if rejected by their American adoptive parents? No social services vetting. American Service personnel were bringing babies home and Americans were making baby shopping trips to Ireland.

The Irish Embassy in Chicago began asking questions about the validity of such adoptions. Monsignor O'Grady avoided questions or gave vague answers. The report even noted that "Monsignor O'Grady made a very poor impression on us. He is very old and rather senile at times...It beats us how he holds down such a job."

The truth is, the system was not really a system at all, but a loose network of priests believing that what Ireland needed was a good purging of illicit souls. That self-righteous belief trumped all legal and even moral questions. "Sign the papers, it's for the good of the child," was their mantra.

In my research I found and feel Child trafficking today preys on impoverished women who have no way to take care of their children. They sell them on the black market with the promise that the child will be given a better life. What disturbs me is the parallels in child trafficking today and the Irish adoption scandal that permeated my own adoption. Certainly, the vast majority of buyers of babies on the Irish black market in these more innocent times had good intentions, motives beyond perversion and debauchery. But who's to know what bad things could happen to them once they were behind closed doors in America without any safety checks.

By comparison, today's adoption process requires in-home assessments and background checks by a third-party. Each Country and State has requirements that must be fulfilled. There are emigration requirements, character witness letters, and financial statements. Assessments are done both on the child and the adoptive parents. But, most importantly, the birth mother reviews profiles of qualified adoptive parents and chooses the parents most suitable for her child. For the twins from Ireland, we were store-bought like chattel. A few signatures, smile for the photos, and we were on the plane, experiencing fears we could not define.

Expediting the process could only be done by a man with connections. And Monsignor Hawkes had them. In the postwar boom that shaped modern California, Monsignor Hawkes was as big as the celebrities who sat in his congregation. He was second-in-command to two cardinals and ran his LA Church for three decades. He brokered real estate deals, built churches, fed the poor, taxed the parishes, and socialized with celebrities and business tycoons. He was a power broker at a time when all eyes were on Hollywood. No one ever went up against him because he had the status and the connections to destroy careers and lives. He even spent time with actor Robert DeNiro, teaching him how to be a priest in a movie based on Hawkes' life. Ironically, one of DeNiro's co-stars in this film, Cyril Cusack had a famous daughter named Sinead, herself married to Jeremy Irons, who had a son out-of-wedlock that she secretly gave up for adoption. It turned out that this boy—a future Irish politician—had an adopted brother who was the secret lovechild of the famous singing priest Father Michael Clearly and his housekeeper. What were the odds on one family adopting two "famous" kids? But Ireland is such a small country.

Hawkes' presence in Ireland signaled his status in the church. He could negotiate with governments who relied on the Church to alleviate the welfare burden of their state. They owed him and he leveraged it. The nuns rolled out the red carpet for him at Temple Hill. It seemed in the history books and articles I poured over his reputation for finding babies for Tinsel Town's parents required a bit of pomp and humble servitude. Hawkes reveled in it. Even a whisper against him would have you re-assigned to poverty-stricken Africa or South America. It explains the power of superiors over lower-level priests, and a clandestine culture of preservation. In July 2017, Archbishop Denis Hart stated: "I'd rather go to prison than report child abuse to police." I believe it was a pervasive stance among priests.

In May of 1961 photos arrived from Ireland of me and my sister posing with Reverend Mother Josepha: purely marketing photos. I look at the photos now and see the consternation on my face, the tight grip this woman had on my wrist. I imagine threatening whispers to "be still and smile." I'm still sad when I see the tears on that little 3-year old's face...me.

On July 28, 1961, we arrived at our new, supposedly forever, home in Saratoga, California. Without ever laying eyes on us, and under the direction of Monsignor Hawkes, we were delivered from one institution to another: the pretend happy home of Bill and Helen Hawkes, a place where we were treated like property. We were the jeweled robes worn by the Pharisees, the whitewash on the sepulchers. I wish I'd been old enough to miss my mother, but I wasn't. Not yet.

Bill Hawkes was a bit short and lean, a very reserved and stern man. At 46 years old he was not going to be the fun; young father toddlers should grow up with. Helen was short, slightly built with perfect hair that was stiff in the style of the day, sitting up off her head. She was pretty. The house was a long, red brick rambler and sat on a big lot with a broad lawn in the back, and lemon trees beyond. It was a neighborhood that spread out and made use of the expansive

California land so available in the 40s and 50s. Shrubs and trees were meticulously trimmed. It was a house you would find in Father Knows Best, everything perfectly in place, the doting wife, the father who arrives home each night, briefcase in hand, to sit in his easy chair waiting for dinner. It was, by all appearances, the American dream.

Two older sisters, the biological twins of Bill and Helen, were well behaved 9-year-olds. They saw us as a curiosity, pets of a sort, something that flew in from Ireland and would be boarding at their house for a while. I don't think they hated or resented us as much as they just ignored us. We settled into our rooms, and I remember just staring about. The walls were an off white and there was a little dresser for clothes, and a closet with vented doors. Funny what you remember as a first impression. Bill and Helen were talking in one room and the sisters were talking in another. My sister and I would have to learn to bond again because we were separated at five months, then brought together just before the adoption. I remember running through the house yelling at my sister to come look at the very curious appliances in the home, especially the toilets. Neighbors dropped by and we stood out in front of Bill and Helen to be examined. The biological sisters giggled at our Irish accents. I think I was embarrassed, or just overwhelmed, but tears welled up in my eyes once again. No one noticed.

Nearly 4 years after she last held us tight, we were still very much in our poor mother's thoughts. A February 6, 1962 letter arrived at the St. Patrick's Guild offices of the Irish Sisters of Charity. It read,

My Dear Sisters, please accept this little gift in
thanksgiving for all your kindness to myself and

twins. I can never thank you enough for being
so understanding towards me. How are the
twins? Did you have any news since they went
to America, as they are never out of my mind. I
don't expect you to answer as I know you are busy,
so maybe you could ring me in my work phone
number. Please pray for me.

Yours respectfully, Betty Mancell.

Betty was desperate to know if we were OK, if the family was kind. Nothing was sent to her for over a year other than the report that the two of us had been sent together to America, a long way from working-class Ireland. There would be no hope of stealing a glance at her children at Catholic school or searching public parks hoping God would grant a miracle. We were on the other side of the world and there wasn't a chance the nuns would ever reveal to my mother where we landed and who we were with.

Later that month, Betty received photos of us, sent by Bill and Helen Hawkes, to the Sisters of Charity, with a letter from the sister in Charge. It read,

Dear Mrs. Mancell,

Thank you very much for your letter and Mass
Card—It was indeed very kind of you to think
of us like this. I've been intending to let you have
these pictures ever since I got them at Christmas,
but I have been very busy. Don't they look happy?
We get glowing accounts of them, both from the

people themselves and the adoption authorities
there—everyone is just thrilled with them—and
why wouldn't they be? We pray for you always—
may God and Mary bless you and guard you
always.

Yours sincerely in J.C.,
Sister in Charge.

Betty shared the precious photos of us with Maura, Catherine, and Eddie, who helped her nearly four years before, when she returned with the babies to Dublin. Betty had spent many visits with Maura when she wasn't working at the Olympic or washing sheets at home. She took long walks with Eilish. Neighbors later told me that the two were a fixture in town, always together, walking everywhere, sitting in the same pew at church. Some mentioned how hard it must have been for Betty to be without a husband and taking care of Eilish and her mother. Those were the last photos Betty was to ever receive of her twins. She never got another report from Helen and Bill, or the Sisters of Charity. What was done was done.

CHAPTER

Five

*I*n the three years before we arrived in Bill and Helen's home my sister and I had been separated from our mother, from each other, brought back together, propped for photographs, and dispatched like a glorified mail order to a new country.

Much research has been done on the psychological damage on our type of early childhood trauma, separation, uncertainty, and lack of affection. My sister became emotionally vulnerable, and I became defiant. Both of us were dependent on this new family structure to survive.

There was clear favoritism shown towards the older biological twins. After our novelty wore off, we were dealt with severely for the smallest infractions. I don't remember exactly at what age I knew we were adopted, but I do remember being scolded in piety when I disobeyed my parents. Or, when I asked why Santa was never as good to my sister and I as he was to the biological sisters. "You should just be grateful we took you in," I was told.

The transition wasn't easy for any of the Hawkes household either; two forty-six-year-old parents and two

9-year-old biological children suddenly sharing their space, their home, with two toddlers could not have been as fun as they'd initially imagined it would be.

Then there was the complex relationship between Bill Hawkes and his younger brother, the celebrity priest. Bill suffered a tremendous inferiority complex when it came to his own brother. His body language changed when Monsignor Hawkes arrived and was treated to the finest meal Helen could muster up, regaling us all with stories of his business prowess, mission from God, associations with Popes, Hollywood stars and famous millionaires. Bill would sit quietly in the corner, the backseat in his own living room. It is in these days, when the photo of Ben and me was taken, me on his lap like some kind of trophy. I remember his hand stroking my thigh. In other visits he would wet his finger and stick it in my ear.

As I grew older my circle of friends widened. We attended elementary school at the local Catholic Sacred Heart School. At home I lived the role of strict servitude, but with friends I adopted another persona. I was fun and always up for a game of kickball, or baseball. My sister was more reserved and withdrawn. My defense mechanism was to push back gently on authoritarian rule, invoke humor and feign innocence. I could survive if I could be defiant and get a laugh. But I was also keenly aware that my life was not what other boys my age were experiencing.

I'd walk home with friends and quietly observe their family dynamics. There was a sharp contrast. The Hawkes' household was extremely strict. I had to ask for permission to get food from the refrigerator or pantry. Baths and showers were infrequently allowed, repeated requests to participate in youth organized sports was dismissed because it was deemed too expensive for children not really part of the family, yet the biological daughters participated in a variety of after school activities, from music lessons to social outings to college prep boarding school.

Punishment for small infractions was demeaning and often physical. Each verbal or physical lashing was accompanied by the same line: "you should be grateful we brought you here from your dirty little orphanage in Ireland. You weren't wanted anywhere else." Other times we were told, "You're not blood so you wouldn't understand."

Helen even told me a number of times that she regretted adopting us. In a fit of anger one day, Helen admitted that she was never in favor of our adoption in the first place. Her life was controlled by the Church, and by the husband she called "Daddy." She was a secret drinker, which was probably the only way she could cope with it all. I remember getting up at around 7am on Sunday mornings. Helen was listening to the radio and drinking a glass of wine. I asked what she was doing? "Listening to the Mormon Tabernacle Choir and having a little wine," she responded. "It brings me peace."

Most days the wine bottle opened up again at three in the afternoon. Keeping up outward appearances took its toll on her.

One memory stands out: we were reciting our Hail Mary's at the dinner table. I was hungry and rushed through the recitation.

"Slow down, Michael," Bill said.

Noting his irritation, I recited it again, at the same speed.

"Slow Down Michael!"

I recited it again, just as fast. Bill ripped the rosary out of my hands and chased me around the house, whipping me with it. I mostly outran him, but he got in a few good licks. I knew I could tire him out. Eventually I sat in a corner and ate when the rest of the family was dismissed. It was a small victory for me.

At an early age, I looked forward to being sent off to college, something Bill and Helen also referred to often. Leaving the family nest, one filled with thorns, is much easier when you have nothing emotionally to lose.

Living in a home devoid of affection only exacerbated my defiant spirit. Perhaps it was a survival instinct. But it did not go over well with the nuns at Sacred Heart Elementary. My guess is, Bill and Helen talked privately with the Nuns and told them I needed to be "set straight." Being the unwanted offspring of a fallen mother and charitably taken into their home, they "deserved" a better child and probably asked that I be made to act like one. They were, after all, paying my tuition. They expected results.

On the surface Bill and Helen were pillars of society. Helen played the organ at the local church and volunteered as the school librarian. And we must not forget, Bill was the brother to Monsignor Hawkes. Reputations were at stake and if I could be reformed their redemption would follow.

Alas, I would only get worse at school. I was paddled often, and treated poorly, like the castoff they believed me to be. I struggled with the tactic of corporeal punishment and authoritarian rule. I would not succumb. It created an inner anger in me that I would have to reconcile years later. So, I spent a lot of time in the Principal's office sitting on my hands because my backside hurt. But the beatings were kind of a badge of honor to me. I took them with a resolute jaw, my hands placed on Mother Superior's desk while she administered sharp whacks like she was beating a rug. Sometimes the skin blistered and broke. But I did not. I would not.

I became a little more brazen as I got older, perhaps because I could sense that I could be the cause of much embarrassment if I put my mind to it. I took advantage. One day, in the fifth grade, I was talking in class. I was a funny kid. Humor hid the pain. Sister Jean had enough. She flung a chalkboard eraser at me. Defiant, I threw it right back, leaving a white stain on her black habit. It was an Irish act of rebellion. Of course, there was the paddle. But like Job, there was also deliverance after the tribulation.

A letter was sent to Bill and Helen. It read, "We the administrators of Sacred Heart Elementary School, are of the opinion that Michael would benefit from attending an alternative school. He is no longer welcome to attend Sacred Heart."

My expulsion was a momentous day of release. No more religious hypocrisy, no paddles, no safety pins in the cuffs of nun's sleeves to encourage me to focus. The nuns would sneak up behind me, put a gentle hand on my shoulder, and with the other hand, crack me across the knuckles with a ruler. Any resistance would result in another prick, another rap. After all, order in God's kingdom has to be enforced, and suffering, I would learn, is part of the plan. I have had a fear of safety pins my whole life. I read an article about babies in Catholic orphanages like the one I grew up in being pinned to their mattresses by their bedclothes so they wouldn't stand in their cribs. Perhaps I have some repressed memory of being put to bed every night that way. And I certainly was afraid of the pins as "gentle persuaders."

By some miracle we were sent to public school. I'm sure it was a big stress relief for Helen and Bill. They were merely trying to survive us then and having us out of Catholic school would save them some embarrassment, and some money. Besides, it could easily be explained away with phrases we often overheard: "well, they're not really our children anyway."

Still, they did sometimes try to make me feel like a part of their family, like outings to the beach on weekends or during the summer holiday—but basically only whenever we were in public, which allowed my parents to play to the gallery as good caretakers. At that early age, I ached for their affection and attention. They poured it on when we were out in the community, and I would wrap myself up in this faux emotional blanket. But it ended behind closed doors.

Sunday was the day we were dressed in stiff clothes and paraded up the center aisle to the pious front pew. I would hear comments about how saintly my parents were to take in two more mouths to feed. I can only imagine the validation of righteousness my parents must've felt. I look back at my craving for their affection and can't help but remember the line from Oliver Twist: "Please sir, may I have some more?" Because when we got home, all appearances of perfection dissolved, and I was either belittled or left entirely alone while the biological heirs to my father's kingdom were doted on.

During the week, Bill would come home and kiss Helen on the cheek. She would address him as Daddy, and then whisper in his ear all the things my sister and I had done wrong that day. I would then sit in abject fear while the clock ticked, and the biological daughters giggled and conversed with *their* parents. Then the words would come from Bill: "Michael, go to your room and wait for me there."

He always gave me a few tortured minutes to dread what was coming next. And really, I mostly never knew what I had done wrong for the day. He'd enter the room, tell me to stand at the foot of the bed. He would stand behind me, reach around and undo my pants and yank them down to my ankles. Slowly he would undo his belt and draw it out like a scourge. Then he would whip me with it, six, seven, eight times across the bare buttocks. It hurt like hell. Even as a ten-year-old, it sent a clear message that he detested me with all his heart.

I do not remember my biological sisters ever being cruel, but it was always understood that they were in a caste above us. It must've really hurt my sister to not have that sisterly bond. She never mentioned it, but her angst and detachment from the family later in life spoke volumes. She, likewise, was treated like chattel.

Rather than mother-daughter outings she was mostly alone at home. One day at the dinner table, Helen whispered to Bill about my sister. The infraction was so insignificant I don't even remember it. I was old enough for the memory to trouble me for years. After a silent dinner, the two of us were sent to our rooms. Bill barked at her: "Go to your room and wait for me there. You know why."

Anxiety rose up in me like a fever, trembling, fight or flight synapses firing on all cylinders. We both trudged to our bedrooms. My sister didn't look at me. She wanted to be strong, or keep everything bottled up, maybe a little of both. I could do nothing but go to my room. I knew any protest would mean a beating for me, too. Or worse, I had this irrational fear that we would be thrown out on to the streets in LA, among the homeless and drug addicts my father pointed out as object lessons.

I sat in my room with my knees pulled up to my chest and listened to my sister screaming. This eleven-year-old girl was being whipped like a prisoner of the Vietcong. I knew exactly what was happening down to every last detail, because Bill was not very creative in his punishments. He pulled down her pants, had her grab hold of the footboard of her bed. Then with his leather belt he beat her across the bare buttocks.

There was no holding back because she was a girl. She got the same amount of stripes as I did. Then with a sinister smirk on his face he told her how lucky she was that he had saved her from the filthy streets of Ireland.

I could only cry silently. I got through it by closing my eyes, but I heard every whip, every word, every heavy breath of his.

We twins shared the secret language of tears. We didn't know how to talk about the pain or what we were feeling. After each beating, the other would sneak into the room and we would cry together; she for me and me for her. We held each other in that tight cocoon and let the tears flow. We had this unspoken pact to suffer for each other.

On sunny summer afternoons, when Bill was at work and Helen was off shopping with the biological daughters, we sneaky twins would climb the hills behind our neighborhood with other children. We were young and craved the playtime other kids in the neighborhood were privileged to enjoy. For us, it was an indulgence that came with a punishment. There was a big tree, and its shade kept the sun from burning the soft grass beneath the branches.

We spent hours chasing each other and throwing tufts of grass, sliding down the hill on our knees and looking out over the suburbs like conquering pirates. For a time, we were unbridled. But we knew what awaited us when we got home.

Dirty knees had no place in the Hawkes' home unless you were praying in the garden. We each got the belt after dinner. Again, we held each other. Sometimes our tears turned to defiant smiles. I don't remember how many times my father released his belt on me. Thank God it was less for my sister.

CHAPTER

Six

Any Southern California visits were centered on seeing Uncle Ben at St. Basil's Church in downtown Los Angeles. Ben had risen in the ranks in the archdiocese and was the pastor of St. Basil's. The now Right Reverend Monsignor Hawkes was also named as the Vicar General of the Archdiocese of Los Angeles. His station still unnerved my father and that frustration was often aimed at me. Monsignor Hawkes was used to people slaving all over him. But he also had a glorified pet in me— and my father was only happy to oblige. After all, wasn't this the purpose of my adoption in the first place? To become whatever fate the Monsignor had in mind for me?

I began to get invitations to visit Monsignor Hawkes at St. Basil's church without the rest of the family. Helen would receive a phone call stating that a plane ticket had been purchased for me and that I would be visiting for a long weekend, or longer during the summer. I would fly alone from San Jose to Los Angeles International airport and get picked up by an archdiocese driver and delivered to the imposing structure of St. Basil's.

At first, those visits were a great adventure. Monsignor Hawkes was often busy and would spend meals and mass with me but would assign a priest or butler to take me to interesting places in Southern California. I went to Disneyland once with the St. Basil's rectory butler. It was strange to cruise around Disneyland with a stoic and reserved servant. I watched families laughing together and siblings jostling for front seats on rides. I spent the day with a butler who didn't seem to be enjoying the park at all. Still, I was grateful for the time away from Bill, his lengthy list of chores and the threat of the belt. Given a choice, I'd rather have been playing baseball with my pals. This was an impressionable time for me. I had learned to feign compliance while around the nuns and the importance of outward appearance from my parents. What I was about to learn was the cost of affection from my uncle.

St. Basil's Church is a grand structure on Wilshire Boulevard. Huge concrete walls interspersed with massive stained-glass windows. It has a modern design that can be seen from a great distance, beckoning the faithful to come. When you walk through the massive doors, you are immediately seized with the size of the building. In the entrance are monstrous 20-foot tall bronze statues of Peter and Paul, which look very menacing to a young boy. Not like historical descriptions of early apostles of Christ, these are more fierce like Goliath, enforcers of the laws of God. When looking at the altar, eyes are drawn to an exceptionally large and modern design of a Cardinal's hat hanging from the ceiling, indicating at one point that Cardinal McIntyre had been in residence at this church. The Stations of the Cross are created as reliefs inside the modern fortress-like concrete towers. Nine-hundred people could comfortably fit in the mahogany pews as Monsignor Hawkes preached his sermon and while saying mass from the elevated loft on the right side of the altar. The 80-foot high concrete slabs command a spectacular presence almost as large as the presence of its pastoral leader. He was a powerful man, a deity himself.

At first the massive wooden doors to the rectory were an impressive sight. It was like entering a castle and my uncle was the king. I imagined the priests at St. Basil's as his servants. He commanded respect and order, but was gentle toward me, not harsh like his brother. His face was thin, lips tight as if they were withholding something. His residence was like that of all great kings; ages of wisdom surrounded him as if he were part of an extensive line of God servants linking directly back to Jesus.

When I was of age, I became an altar boy, under the tutelage of Monsignor Hawkes. More than once he sat down next to me in the rectory on a hand carved wooden bench, put his hand on my knee and drew his face uncomfortably close to mine. "You could be a priest," he'd whisper. "It's a blessed life."

I was serving as an altar boy at mass at St Basil's Church for Monsignor Hawkes who was seen as big a star as the celebrities who sat in the first pew. Monsignor Hawkes was to them the incarnation of Christ himself, and their ticket to redemption. They made hefty donations.

The notion that I could be in line for the same stature intrigued me. I had not yet discovered girls, so the misgivings of celibacy had not yet entered my mind. I was set on the track at the most junior position, one entrusted to holy children, not misfits like myself. I didn't question why he chose me. I naively bought into the promises.

The grandiose idea of me joining the priesthood was a very welcome notion for Bill and Helen. It would "sanctify" their "sacrifice." As for me, I could see God's purpose in it. Perhaps, I often told myself, it was the very reason I was adopted. It was a way to finally gain the approval I had so sorely missed.

I was too young to understand that the Catholic Church was a system of punishments without reward. But the ever-present crucifix was obviously a reminder that disobedient children would similarly suffer for their infractions if they didn't toe the line. And if that didn't work, there was my father's belt across my backside, or I was whipped with a rosary. God, at that time, seemed an abstract and commanding ruler, a great punisher. I hoped with the adoration of a pre-pubescent boy, to someday be on his good side.

Structured religion seemed an escape from my second-class existence. The complex of emotions I was feeling led to one primal need: to be loved. My uncle the Monsignor was not strict in the physical sense but rather encouraging. His love for me was not complete, but it was more than I got at home. St. Basil's was a kingdom within reach. Perhaps it was here that God would even the score. I admit that part of me wanted to snub Bill and Helen with my own righteous indignation.

On one of my visits to St. Basil's, I was told that I had been registered for a week-long summer immersion at St. John's Catholic Seminary in Camarillo. It might have been a week away from the emotional rigor of keeping my guard up at home, but it was also a week away from afternoons playing pickup games of baseball. Again, my emotions were mixed.

The Catholic camp was designed for young men interested in the priesthood. It was in a campus setting and designed like a series of recruiting seminars where we were instructed in ritual and doctrine, and discussed the purpose of celibacy and the profession as a servant of Christ.

That week left me more confused than ever. Part of it was my expectations going in. I wanted leadership training so I could run my own church, become king like my uncle Ben. It seemed a good profession. But mixing the sacrifice and goodness of Christ with the pursuit of power and wealth left me conflicted. The discussions of doctrine were disturbing enough in their penance-based theology.

At exercise periods there were fights on the football field. I watched two older boys go at it without restraint. Fists flying in rage, blood and spit and profanity flying from angry mouths. The memory is frozen with me, like the statue of Hercules and Diomedes grappling to the death. It's a frightening sculpture, with Hercules about to throw Diomedes over a cliff and Diomedes gripping Hercules by the genitals. I remember the sculpture from one of Monsignor Hawkes' art books. Terrifying.

It didn't seem right that boys preparing for the gospel of Christ were thus engaged trying to destroy each other. It was all very confusing to me; all I wanted was to be good, to be loved. Even at that youthful age I could sense the contradictions.

I would lay awake at night wondering where my mother was. Why had I not heard from her? Was she so fallen that the devil and his minions had chained her in some dungeon deep in the bowels of hell? Such are the thoughts of a boy surrounded by images of crucifixion and flagellation. One of the images at priest camp was of Adam and Eve being cast out of the Garden of Eden by an angry God. I cried when I saw it.

I couldn't sleep at night. I feared this camp was making me into the very monsters that tormented me. A God who punished. Nuns who pricked young students with pins. Fathers who beat children in perverse ways. And worst of all, the cast offs like my mother who had no chance at returning. I was a mess of emotions. I wept for my mother. She was tossed away for sins that I could not understand but somehow owned. I was suffering with her. What began as a pathway to joy ended in sadness. I just could not see myself becoming a priest. And yet, I felt like I had no control over my own destiny.

CHAPTER

Seven

My first night at Ben's residence in the Cathedral, I slept in a small room adjacent to his. Before going to bed Ben entered my room and told me to shower. "You must be a clean boy," he said. He watched me shower, and patted me dry with a towel. He put his hand on my shoulder, stroked my back down to my buttocks and pressed his finger into my anus. "There, clean inside and out." He stepped away and left me alone to wonder what just happened.

It is clear to me now why I was of such interest to Monsignor Hawkes in Ireland. He had an insatiable appetite for young boys and I was part of the farm club: the raising up of sacrificial lambs to his altar of perversion. His affections for me, his kindness, his promises of a better life, the trip to Disneyland—it had all been a cunning scheme. My very existence was to satisfy his depravity. But at the time, I was just a confused boy whose emotions were being tamped down deeper and deeper into his soul.

Before the abuse began, the hustle and bustle of Los Angeles was an exciting escape from the then sleepy

Santa Clara Valley of Northern California. It was a great adventure. There wasn't much ability on behalf of Bill and Helen to refuse the Monsignor. They appeared unwilling to challenge anything my uncle suggested. It was never a request. It was always a directive. They complied and saved their attention for the biological daughters. I was on my own in Ben's world, and I knew it.

The rectory, the priests' residence, was also within the building of St. Basil's. I was impressed by how well the inhabitants ate in their dining room, but slightly unnerved at how the poor would see these extravagant meals. On occasion, I was taken to visit the Cardinal's residence to meet Cardinal McIntyre.

Cardinal McIntyre bent over to look me in the eye. His skin was pale and he seemed an old sage in his cedar smelling robes. He was then a man of many years and had been the long-time mentor to Monsignor Hawkes. As a boy I was looking for father figures, Cardinal McIntyre seemed a good man. He encouraged me to do well in school and to grow into God's calling for me. But as I got older and the liberal world erupted around us, Cardinal McIntyre held onto ultra-conservative views and was asked a number of times by local priests to refrain from making racist remarks. There were marches by blacks and Hispanics protesting his views and he suspended Father William Dubay who had become vocal against the Cardinal, and even called for his removal because McIntyre wouldn't support the civil right movement. Again, it felt like the leaders in the Catholic Church were free to pick and choose who moved up Jacobs ladder toward Heaven and who would be held down.

As the day expired at St. Basil's, the priests retired to their rectory to, what most would think, is an ideal time to ponder, pray, meditate on their service to the vulnerable, and prepare for the next days in ministry to God's children. This was not the case with Monsignor Hawkes. At St. Basil's rectory, young men lived in fear of a side of this priest that was dark and foreboding.

My room for the night was not a safe haven. Budding priests were not surrounded by the angels of heaven. There were fallen ones too, which made sleep exceedingly difficult. Dreams became nightmares. The room was under the control and desires of my uncle, who could come through the door at any moment, the priest in his silk boxers.

There was no night lamp. And in that darkness, the wrestle with evil became real, flesh on flesh. At 12-years-old I had been carefully groomed for this room. In that darkness Monsignor Hawkes, the pious, most powerful priest in Los Angeles, would jerk open the door stride into my room and tear open my soul. Frozen in fear, held fast by demons of what would be if I resisted? I lay in total horror until he was finished with me. The episodes caused nightmares the rest of my life. It was unspeakable. It still is. My uncle was a monster, a medieval gargoyle at the gates of St. Basil's devouring children.

The heavy darkness of his soul pinned me to my bed long after he had left the room. Each weekend tore deeper into my emotions until I could no longer feel happiness, wonder, or awe a child should experience. Instead, I sobbed uncontrollably.

In my young mind I could only believe that this was the life assigned to me by a cruel God. That powerful men act in his name publicly and are granted the perversions of their souls as reward.

By day, Monsignor Hawkes was a man who dined with members of the elite of Los Angeles Catholic and Hollywood royalty. At night he was an abusive, base monster, satisfying himself on young altar boys preparing communion.

An example of the grotesque and lecherous nature of this man was constantly illustrated in his behavior in the sacristy of St. Basil's church. The sacristy is the room right off the altar where the priest who was to say mass would compose himself for this most holy service. Implements of the mass were prepared and altar boys would arrange the chalices for holy mass. Carefully, the 12 to 14-year-old boys would place the communion wafers inside the chalices. The wine also was set-aside in their assigned chalices, which were gilded in the finest gold and silver.

Monsignor Hawkes demanded absolute reverence and perfection to the utmost detail. Altar boys would enter the sacristy in their cassocks, long black robes over their clothes. It was also the sacristy where, as a boy, I experienced the brutality and unholy, unfathomable acts of Monsignor Hawkes. As myself and the other altar boys worked diligently, readying everything for the mass and preparing the altar, our hope was to receive a pious nod from the Monsignor that everything looked great and we were now ready to walk out from the sacristy to the altar, reverently with fingers and hands clasped together.

With a trembling hand I would light the candles and return to the sacristy where Monsignor Hawkes would finish preparing his cassock and vestments for the mass. With just minutes to go, and before walking out as a contingency in front of the congregation, Monsignor Hawkes, would walk up to us innocent altar boys and under the gaze of the crucifix, shove us against the wall and undo our cassocks, reach down our pants and grab hold of genitalia. Those not being molested would stand in absolute fear, unable to move, in shocked horror that this lewdness was happening. The boys I served with were as frightened as I. We never spoke about what happened in the sacristy, but we often cried. Tears filled our eyes and we looked at each other unable to speak. Unable to explain the emotions we were feeling. To speak up was to lose everything.

When he was finished, Monsignor Hawkes would smile impishly, straighten our cassocks and mass would proceed. "All right boys, hands together, fingers toward Heaven, Let's do this right," he would command.

The mass that was to follow was completed in abject fear—the expressions on our faces mistaken by the patrons as one of stoic reverence.

The memory of this, and presumably other altar boy victims of Monsignor Hawkes, caused unimaginable terror for years.

To be threatened with a complete cutting off from humanity seemed to me like a sentence to hell, as an adopted person from a fallen mother, who had for years heard: "I wish we had never adopted you."

Monsignor Hawkes had been successfully gaining my trust and love since I was three-years-old. I had looked up to the Monsignor as both an uncle and a priest who commanded respect from everyone. A man of that position could punish you or even have you made an outcast if you did not obey his every perverted whim. And yet, I was fortunate that I could leave after a weekend at St. Basil's. Other altar boys who resided in the parish were not so lucky. Victims were equally vulnerable, including children of immigrants from South America, who were beholden to Monsignor Hawkes as their sponsor. Their lives and the lives of their parents depended on the Monsignor. Even if the abuse were to become known, these families would keep it a secret out of fear.

CHAPTER

Eight

*O*ne of my duties as an Altar Boy was to accompany the priests to the rectory with the weekend's collections at St. Basil's. Monsignor Hawkes and the other priests gathered around a large round table, on which they would dump out all the money from the offerings from the weekend's masses—the widow's mites.

I watched as they silently sat at the table, counting large stacks of paper money and coins. The priests counted their money as if it were poker winnings. But there were no IOUs here, only hard cash. There would be thousands of dollars in the offerings. After the count, a large cabinet wall was opened; there on the shelves was the most extensive collection of expensive liquor. My own father's treasured liquor collection paled in comparison. The liquor was ceremoniously poured and passed out to the priests. These supposedly pious men of God gleefully gulped down expensive liquor bought with the parishioner's hard-earned money.

While the abuse happened in private, either in the dark, or with the Monsignor alone with altar boys, this gathering of priests like pirates seemed brazenly anti-Christian.

St. Basil's, which stood proudly in the archdiocese of Los Angeles, might have been seen as a monument to God, but to me it was a whitewashed sepulcher, pure on the outside and full of rot on the inside. The Sunday scenes brought to mind the scripture:

Beware of the scribes, which desire to walk in long robes, and love greetings in the markets, and the highest seats in the synagogues, and the chief rooms at feasts...

Back in Saratoga, my parents proudly displayed photos of the good Monsignor, with the Pope at the Vatican in the entryway. (Photos of the biological daughters were next, and around the corner, down the hall were pictures of my sister and I). Bill and Helen, despite all their shortcomings and misaligned motives, could never have imagined that the center of their worship was so dark and debased.

Other questions arose around the rituals themselves, in particular the gilded robes of the Cardinals and Priests on Sunday. If you put a curious boy in Catholic school he is going to ask questions about incongruities. "Christ never wore a gilded robe with gold and jewels, why did the Cardinals?" Such questions would earn you stripes at the Hawkes compound.

I kept my suffering deep inside. Each weekend as I entered St. Basil's through those enormous doors, I passed by the Stations of the Cross. Here was Christ's suffering carved dramatically in stone. Each portico in my life, from pre-pubescence to adulthood seemed to be one more station of suffering. I physically had felt the stripes of my father's belt across my back, or the paddle on my behind. I understood the distraught expressions of Jesus and it felt that I was destined to be him, in his suffering, forever. I couldn't even approach him and ask why? No access was granted to Jesus except through Mary. It seemed impossible to my mind at that time that I would ever know a Jesus that didn't represent suffering. I was bound by a Saint with dark eyes who would never let me pass.

On one weekend I was told to take a shower before dinner in the tile bathroom that adjoined his bedroom at St. Basil's. Monsignor Hawkes walked in wearing only his silk boxer shorts. He grabbed me, and threw me violently through the door and onto the bed in his room. His arm was across my neck and there was nothing I could do to stop what he was doing. By the mercy of God, I blacked out and have no memory of what happened next. It was the most aggressive he had been with me, more than the fondling. It was brutal and I cannot recover the bulk of what happened. I was later told by my therapist that this is not unusual. Many victims of abuse black out during traumatic events. There is also the chance that throwing me across the room stunned me, hit my head in some way. I don't know.

To cross the wires of a developing brain is to inflict lifelong damage. Many of the Sandusky victims at Penn State and Boy Scouts of America became drug addicts, or worse, pedophiles themselves. Most common is anxiety, depression, and a disassociation with self. It means the victim feels worthless and helpless, and therefore becomes a target over and over. Later in life they struggle with relationships, self worth issues, eating disorders, and suicidal thoughts.

My defense mechanism was to develop a sense of humor that allowed me to make light of life and distance myself from emotional pain. The physical pain was a little harder to ignore. Getting whipped by my father with a Rosary or leather belt welted my backside and the tender skin on my lower back. But I was determined to not let it break me.

I soon learned the rules of living a double life. My father was a prominent community member with an immaculate yard, perfect children, and a doting wife. Behind closed doors he saw his adopted children as a duty thrust upon him by a brother who had risen in status far beyond what he could have imagined. His resentment was tangible. When Monsignor Hawkes came over to the house, the finest meals were prepared. He told stories of celebrities and my older sisters delighted in his halo. My father was sullen. Helen was the perfect host. When Ben left, she kept up airs at the school. But soon after the bell rang, she hit the liquor cabinet to cope. For that I am grateful. It gave me afternoons with my friends. I harbored dark secrets. But who could I tell?

Monsignor Hawkes left a promising accounting career to join the priesthood. I personally think he did this because he had lusts to satisfy and because he could see a path to power. He wore expensive black suits, gold cufflinks, and belonged to two Country Clubs where he rubbed shoulders with the rich and famous. Maybe Bill's resentment was rooted in the hypocrisy of his brother. I will never know. My father was a stern man who never let emotions show, unless he was angry. His brother Ben built the largest Archdiocese in the Country, larger than the one in Chicago. He bought and sold real estate for the Catholic Church amassing a kingdom worth over a billion dollars in the seventies. He oversaw the financial decisions of 1300 priests. Most were terrified of him. Orphans were just another commodity, a profitable enterprise. His pious pitch convinced governments on both sides of the ocean to facilitate transactions with little or no oversight.

The bartering for souls was as evil to me as the abuse itself. Helpless mothers put their faith in Monsignor Hawkes, recipients paid handsomely for babies. And the Church turned a blind eye to the abuse as if the acts were some kind of reward for priests who served well. Altar boys who were abused became priests who abused. In their own words, they provided comfort for young boys the way they had received comfort.

Not much of this was apparent as I grew into my teenage years. But a lifetime of research has uncovered a secret society within the Catholic Church that not only facilitated and enabled a system of abuse, it empowered abusers by protecting them from accusations, moving them to new parishes, and ignoring the victims. The house of God had its basement of catacombs, connecting lust to innocents, slaying them anew. Between 1950 and 2016, 6,700 priests and other clergy have been accused of sexual abuse (source: BishopAccountability.org). Who knows how many victims that represents? Orphan placement was just one way of putting boys into the system.

In psychological terms we experience over-anxiety when trauma breeds in us no escape from our destructive thoughts. I was trapped among the gilded priests and drowning in the suffering of Christ for what I could not understand. Mary, the mother of Christ, seemed to be a helpless bystander, watching me sink into despair with her hand raised in the sign of blessing, a way of saying *good luck getting through this. Goodbye.*

I was glad to leave St. Basil's and come home, sort of.

The outside of our house was immaculate. Bill kept the yard and the small orchard perfectly trimmed. There was no sign of anything out of place for the passersby or the neighbors.

My Saturday mornings and many afternoons were spent trimming the lawn and the bushes, raking fallen leaves, and tending to the fruit trees, manicuring every corner. Of course the biological sisters had little work to do. I had come to accept the hierarchy in our family. The biological daughters were in High School. They often spent midmornings on Summer Saturdays sunbathing in the backyard smelling of coconut tanning oil while I worked in the garden sweating profusely and stunk like the manure I was spreading. My twin sister was working inside of the house with Helen as her overseer. The irony of the two dirty orphans working while the two princesses languished was like a scene in a Greek painting. Goddesses over here. Servants over there. It signaled a virtue that we could not attain and one that the golden heiresses were free to flaunt.

The rose bushes were Bill's to trim. He did so with patience and every Saturday he brought in a handful of perfectly cut blossoms for Helen. When we were done, I hosed off my face and hands and was free to wander down the street to a friend's house: the smoke-filled sanctuary of the Chrisman home. No friends were allowed at the Hawkes home. But I was free on occasion to go off with friends.

The Chrisman home was always my first destination. Saturday afternoons Mrs. Chrisman greeted me at the door, usually in a housecoat mothers wore in those days, whilst doing chores. My friend Rob was an only child. But he was far from a lonely child. He was the sole recipient of his parents' affection. "How are you today, Michael?" Mrs. Chrisman would greet me. "Nice to see you." She would touch me on the arm or shoulder as I came in and it felt electric, almost cleansing. Rob would be in the family room with his dad. I could hear them laughing when I entered. There was never much laughter in my house. They sat on an overstuffed couch and Mr. Chrisman was always puffing on a pipe. I'd be transfixed watching him carefully pack it, then put the flame of the match to the bowl and puff gently. I watched as the smoke rose from the pipe in an almost hypnotic manner. Even today, the smell of pipe tobacco relaxes me, as if I have just settled down in a safe place after being chased by wolves through the night.

We'd watch football games and Rob's father would provide commentary, often humorous. He jostled with his son over jokes between puffs. His way of talking with his teeth clenched tight around the pipe was comical and I remember laughing, but not out loud. Laughing boisterously in my house was a sin and I worked hard to keep it inside, even at Rob's.

When the game was over we'd head out on the front lawn. Mr. Chrisman was a husky, Hemingway type man with a gray beard; his moustache was stained yellow from the ever-present pipe. He would take a broad stance on the lawn like a big bear and challenge us. "OK boys, let's see who can take the old man down!"

We would run at him, gangly boys with no weight to them yet. We'd bounce off his belly and sometimes team up on the same leg. He'd peel us off and hang us upside down before letting us scamper away like squirrels. We would horse around or throw the football back and forth until Mrs. Chrisman stepped onto the front porch and announced dinner. I was always invited to stay, but never allowed to by Bill and Helen. It was an affront to them to let other people feed their kids, especially the orphans in their charge. Feeding and clothing the orphans was a solemn, pious duty, one that Bill was as careful to cultivate as the roses in the yard.

It was Mr. Chrisman who took me to my first professional baseball game in San Francisco. I still remember walking into the stadium, an open-air cathedral. We lounged and cheered and ate sacred hotdogs. It's the best memory of my childhood, time spent with a real dad and a good friend worshipping human accomplishment. I remember wishing that I could live there, in that moment, at the ballpark, forever. No matter who was playing, the sounds, the smells, even the corny organ felt a world away from my real life. Here were people, ordinary people, laughing. That alone was so foreign to me. Boys were running up and down the stairs, fathers were drinking beer and cokes in the humid evening. The bat would crack and every person in the whole stadium froze and watched. That was one of the memories that held me together.

Down the street was another boy my age, Chris. If Rob was off at the hardware store or a ballgame with his father, I would keep walking until I came to Chris' house. His parents were very relaxed about parenting; they were often gone for long chunks of time on Saturdays, and that left the two of us to live by our own rules. Not that it was Lord of the Flies, but Chris had a television and comic books, two things not allowed at my house. He also had ice cream in the freezer and Captain Crunch cereal in the cupboard, two indulgences that were against the strict, healthy diet Helen provided. Besides, Hawkes' money was for Hawkes' children. Something fallen children didn't qualify for. We got our mess of porridge, it was all we deserved. By then, it was all I expected.

Chris would get out the blender, called an Osterizer in those days, pack it with ice cream, milk, and chocolate sauce, give it a good blend, top off the glass with a handful of sugar cereal and head to the TV room for breakfast. It was the oasis for the lost boys of Peter Pan. The TV ran cartoons, while we drank milkshakes and read Mad Magazine. Bill would be aghast at such hedonistic behavior. But to a boy who was whipped by his father and molested by the most powerful priest in LA, it was Heaven. More than that, it was what kept me sane.

There were times in my emotionally haywire adolescence that alcohol from the Hawkes' liquor cabinet seemed the only answer. But I couldn't do it. I watched people from the Hawkes compound consume it all too often to cope. I was looking for door number three and that's where I found my boyhood friends. They were my sanity. In their families, I could see a glimpse of another life, a life that God or Bob Barker was somehow showing me so that I could survive. Mad Magazine was my inspired text, and the smell of pipe tobacco the cleansing incense of my boyhood.

I do have a few good family memories from my childhood. One memory of my father still sticks with me. It was a moment when I glimpsed his humanity. I remember as a boy we went to Hawaii on vacation. We had a hotel right on the beach. Bill and Helen seemed good-natured for a change, less weighed down. My older sisters were with us and had not yet left home. I had a terry cloth jacket to protect me from the sun. I also had sunglasses.

My dad and I were standing on the balcony, looking out at the waves while we waited for the women to get ready. It was mid-morning and breezy. I had secretly packed my favorite toy—a GI Joe with a parachute. I stood holding it on the balcony, wondering if I dare show it to my father.

"What's that you've got?" he asked.

I kind of panicked, thinking he would take it away. I held it up for him to look at. He smiled. "Well let's see if it works. Go down to the beach and I'll drop it down to you."

I ran out of the room and down the stairs. Bill unraveled the parachute and dangled it over the balcony. GI Joe grimaced at me. His arms bulged. Bill let him drop, expecting to see him float onto the sand. I ran down the beach to retrieve him, but the wind kicked up and GI Joe slowly floated out to sea. God was mocking me again, I felt.

I looked up and saw my father pucker his face, shrug his shoulders, and go back in the room. I watched as GI Joe disappeared for good. I remember feeling a sense of loss, but mostly relieved that my father wasn't angry with me. Sometimes that's as much hope as I got: small drops of indifference.

CHAPTER

Nine

As I grew out of being an Altar Boy, the sexual abuse stopped. Life with Bill and Helen remained strained. I had gotten too big for Bill to use the strap on me so he resorted to ignoring me. Helen was alone in her own house with children she did not want. She looked forlornly out the window, missing her daughters. One day, I was doing homework on the couch and Helen suddenly turned around from the window and stared at me. Her expression was one of defeat. Her hand shook as she raised a glass of wine to her lips. "I wish we'd never adopted you," she said calmly. It was something she'd said before in frustration, but this time it stung more than the leather belt.

When I was a boy, I secretly wished Helen would stop Bill from whipping me. I pleaded with her to not let him whip my twin sister. I had glimpsed the kindness on her face when her daughters arrived home. I knew she had the heart to put a stop to it, I just always believed she didn't have the courage. Now I knew she didn't. She felt the same way about me as Bill did. It hurt me to the core.

That night, I went to the Chrisman's. I ate dinner
with them. They laughed, and ate on the couch and Mr.
Chrisman looked at me as if he knew my whole life. He
stroked his beard. "Nice to have you for dinner, Michael."
I just nodded. A two-minute walk from where I was, my
sister was eating alone with Bill and Helen. No one spoke
except for Helen. She repeated the same cold sentence to
her that she had said to me: "I wish we never adopted you."
It is guilt-laden memory I will never get over.

I arrived after dinner. I was 16-years-old. Bill called
to me: "Michael, meet me in your room." I took two steps
into the kitchen, looked at him sitting at the table. When
he looked up at me I just shook my head. He took a deep
breath. He was defeated. There would be no beating.

A few weeks later I was invited to meet Monsignor
Hawkes to talk about college. I landed in time for us to
have dinner together. We ate expensive meals while rich
and famous club members greeted Monsignor Hawkes.
They touched him on the shoulder as if some of his
power and virtue might rub off on them. We talked a little
about college, about his expectations, about a Catholic
scholarship. He told me to do my part and get grades that
would not embarrass him. I flew home early, before Mass
on Sunday.

I admit that I hoped in coming to see the Monsignor
that I would get a car. After all, the biological daughters
each received a brand new Mustang on their birthday,
paid for by Monsignor Hawkes through some wealthy
benefactor. My sister and I were never allowed to drive
the family car, ever. We were even denied the required
permission of Bill and Helen to get drivers licenses. The
hope, even as small as it was, that the Monsignor would

grant me the same wish he had the sisters was another false dream.

Maybe it was because I was getting older and wiser to the world around me but it was now clear there were two worlds living under one roof. My non biological sisters could have a car, a boyfriend, a life of freedom and I got the belt for uttering a swear word or stealing a slice of bread. My twin sister and I were not even allowed to open the fridge to get a can of soda or put a slice of bread in the toaster. Our lives were separate, the curtain was drawn between us.

As If that disparity between the Irish orphans and the two biological daughters wasn't enough, Bill won a brand new Pinto at his local parish bazaar; no doubt he bought up a lot of tickets to make himself look good to the community. As fortune would have it, he won. If the Monsignor wasn't good for a car, this Pinto must be recompense. A pinto. It was not a Mustang, and I was willing to share with my sister. But Bill wasn't having it.

A tow truck arrived the day after the Pinto was delivered to the house. Bill had already sold the car. I was crestfallen and asked him why? He simply told me, "You'll never drive one of my cars. Never."

The message was clear: *"I'm done with you. Two more years until you are an adult and you are on your own."* It seemed to me that the more successful Monsignor Hawkes became, the dourer Bill became. He was unhappy. Helen was unhappy. Their girls went off to college leaving two dirty Irish orphans living in their home. The magic of piety had worn off and Bill and Helen could not wait for us to leave. The blessed daughters came home from their all expense-paid colleges (Catholic scholarships arranged by Ben) when they pleased.

CHAPTER

Ten

Being abused robs you of rational thought. Memories good and bad are blanketed. Today they call it PTSD. Back then I only knew it as life. Nightmares. Headaches. That feeling like something is gnawing at your nerves. I just lived with it.

In my teenage years I was enamored with cars. I loved the horsepower and the sound and the thought of roads that led away. I harbored dark thoughts and memories that made my nerves ache. I wanted to be in love. I didn't know how. My friends talked about girls in hopeful ways, kisses, making-out—innocent stuff boys dream about. I could not escape my first sexual experience as one of coercion, abuse, emotional destruction. How could I take a girl on a date, experience the electricity of holding hands for the first time, the heart palpitations that come with knowing a girl likes you, that she wants you to be vulnerable with her as you tread carefully the path of trust and touch when a lecherous priest had touched me before her?

I turned my affection to cars. And my experience mirrors the rite of passage I was called to pass through.

In some cultures, the rite of passage from childhood to manhood requires circumcision. Others require killing a lion, spending weeks in the wilderness alone. In Ireland it may be the first pint of Guinness with your father. In rural California, it was the teenage road trip, a day driving on winding roads with the roar of an engine at your command. Sounds better than circumcision as a teenager. The speed, the getaway, the power, and freedom were intoxicating. So I filled the emotional void of dating in high school with hours looking at cars.

My neighbor, Mr. Titus had a 1945 MG. It was British green. The hood folded up to expose a simple engine that rumbled and sometimes coughed in protest. I was in love. I would watch Titus for hours, tinkering. I wanted one in the worst way and would fall asleep at night dreaming of the British racing green color.

When the engine was tuned, Titus would take me on long rides through the dry California terrain. The top was down. The wind was coarse. There was more engine than car and that made it feel like you were riding on the very engine itself. And best of all, it was loud enough to discourage conversation. How do you talk about love? I couldn't. I was a master of small talk. But that ran thin after a few quips. Riding along with my mouth open to the wind dried my mouth and stifled any desire to talk. I was happy.

We roared along, Titus as the charioteer. He was another father figure to me, strong and mechanically inclined. He knew how to use tools and he knew not to ask me too many questions. He knew what I really needed was the occasional escape from reality. We returned with wind burned eyes. That's a good thing when you don't want to look back. And pain sometimes reminds you that you are still alive and not numbed to the future.

Monsignor Hawkes still loomed larger than life. What unnerved me most was when he visited; he would wink at me, as if we had a secret.

In our garage was a 1967 Lincoln Continental that used to belong to the Cardinal of Los Angeles, Cardinal McIntyre. I remember the suicide doors, the long, heavy vehicle that seemed to sag under the weight of everything it had carried over the years. Climbing into the backseat of that car was like climbing into a prison bus. I sank down low in the seat. My father drove slowly, his stern face visible in the rearview mirror. The car swayed when it turned. The very weight of it seemed like it would sink us all into the underworld.

My two older sisters raced back and forth from expensive colleges in sports cars, tuition arranged by the Monsignor, cars paid for by the Monsignor, happiness paid for by the Monsignor. It wore on Bill. Driving to church on Sundays we passed Mr. Titus and his open garage. I would look out the window from the back seat of the prison bus while Mr. Titus tuned the carburetor. There would be a Sunday afternoon drive, and I would miss it.

Sometimes the Mustang twins would roar up the highway home from their universities to join us for church. I think I had grown to a point where I didn't expect to be treated equally, that I saw the disparity in my family as unassailable, and that sometime, I would be the one behind the wheel of that MG. Until then, I was handcuffed in the back seat of a dark Lincoln that used to belong to the Cardinal, the overseer of a good flock and a system of perversion and deceit. I often wonder how he kept his emotional and moral balance.

In the meantime, Monsignor Hawkes was building his kingdom and sponsoring new fodder for his lusts. He ruled over an Archdiocese that served two and a half million people. He brokered deals, one in Chinatown closed a parochial school and sold off the land for over $8 million to Chinese developers. He wore a gold watch on his next visit, a gift from the developers. His lust for boys was only matched by his lust for power. His impish smile concealed secret backdoor dealings at the exclusive Los Angeles Country Club.

I'm not a theologian or historian; and I make no excuse for the Catholic Church, or the Irish Government, or the cultural prejudice perpetuated by the society my mother grew up in, and that I became a victim of. What keeps me up at night is knowing that one or two people in places of influence could have spoken up, and didn't. Their silence is complicit in the abuse and oppression of thousands of children and single mothers.

How did an institution become so powerful, and so intimidating?

The history of the Catholic Church and its interrelationship with monarchs and governments offers some understanding of how a quest for power and control overtook the teachings of Jesus. I have great admiration for the early Christians, and their martyrs. Amid the persecution they still held fast to their beliefs, even in the face of torture and death. Christianity grew and Constantine, vying for political power, galvanized the different Christian sects in the council at Nicaea and canonized the doctrine. The Church was a legitimate organization and through the following centuries played a significant role as a political and military organization in the name of preserving the people of God. Monarchies were interwoven with the Church that reached across borders. The crusades were meant to beat heathen nations into submission—convert or die. Christianity in the Roman Empire required all to renounce other cultural traditions and beliefs. The wars over Jerusalem are sad tales of bloodstained streets as Jews, Muslims, and Christians sought control. What makes a place holy is more than one religious sect laying claim to it. Then all hell breaks loose defending it in the name of different Gods and birthrights.

The first threats to Christianity came from outside political forces. So the Catholic Church became political, a master influencer on the world stage. But then the threat came from within. Different Christian sects, The Reformation and branches Protestantism, the enlightenment, all dark influences aimed at destroying the Church. The Catholic Church took a defensive position to sustain power, influence, and piety. Its alignment with governments in Europe connected Church and state in a way that the American Constitution aimed to prevent.

In the words of Lord Acton: "power tends to corrupt and absolute power corrupts absolutely." The first time I heard this phrase was during the Nixon Watergate scandal. Its origin relates directly to the Church having too much power. Lord Acton (1887) was arguing for a more accurate accountability of the Church leadership during the Spanish Inquisition. Until then, the Church held them blameless. Lord Acton wrote to Bishop Creighton arguing that the holders of higher positions should be held to higher standards, not the opposite, which is what the Catholic Church was doing. The belief was that a holy calling empowered you to act above the law. In his correspondence, Lord Acton bravely states: "There is no worse heresy than that the office sanctifies the holder of it." This is the crux, the context I was looking for. Leadership in the Catholic Church sanctified each other in their sins, perpetuating the abuse, forgiving each other, and continuing the practice. I believe Irish government officials were doing the same, placing children in what was akin to child trafficking in cahoots with the Catholic Church without accountability to a third-party because the process was "sanctified." To me, that's heresy. The fruits bear out the roots of the evil. Absolute power corrupts absolutely. I would search my soul for a way to forgive but could not identify anything human to petition. The abuse was systemic. The only person I could try to reconcile with would be my father. It would take years to reach the point where I understood him. But first, I had to be on my own.

I felt like a liberated POW when I went off to Community College. I knew I wouldn't get a scholarship to USC the way the Mustang twins did. Still, I'm sure the Monsignor paid for it with a Catholic scholarship of some kind. But I'm guessing the community college was too close to home and Bill and Helen needed more distance from the fallen children they'd adopted.

I was told a new college was chosen for me. Ben was pulling all the strings in my life.

Bill seemed to be adrift and unattached. He spent a lot of time in his garden, pruning what he could control. Helen would be two hours into cocktail hour by the time he got home from work. I know that he adored her. He adored his two older girls. But he was incomplete. Too much of his life had been managed for him. He didn't own all of it the way he probably dreamed he would have.

Maybe he felt chained to the Catholic Church and its unwritten rules of behavior. Maybe he felt diminished by the stature of his younger brother Ben who seemed to be on track to Sainthood. He was withdrawn and I'll never know how he felt in those years before we both left.

Monsignor Ben Hawkes arranged for me to attend college in the Rocky Mountains, which was not exactly the prestigious school he had arranged for the two biological girls. I received a Catholic scholarship. No surprise there. My major was chosen for me: Business Administration.

A few months later I was on a plane flying away from California. I want to say that I felt a mix of emotions. But that would be something I learned in a book or a movie. What I really felt was nothing. I was chained to memories I could not escape. I had no real father. I missed my sister. But a great fear of our father prevented us from sharing our feelings with each other. It's the one loss in my life that I miss the most, a closeness with my blood sister. But we were both too emotionally damaged to fully connect.

Flying over the Rocky Mountains I felt unmoored, in a good way. It was the first time I had been on a plane when I wasn't flying toward an abusive weekend, or returning from one to a place I would be ignored or derided. I laughed to myself at the memory of Bill chasing me around the house when I was 10-years-old, whipping me with a rosary. There would be none of that at this new school. I also watched the clouds go by and remembered the long drives in the MG with Mr. Titus. I dreamed of restoring a car after college. What I didn't dream of was snow and cold. My first lesson in living on my own was to dress like the natives.

I was Natty Bumppo, thrown into a new frontier, a dual personality from competing societies forging bravely ahead in a vanishing wilderness. I was determined to leave the past behind. College was the perfect doorway. Rather than the Leatherstocking tales, this chapter of my life could be titled the flip-flop tales. I was the California boy. I had tales from far away. I attended their social gatherings and observed their ways.

And I made a lot of friends. I was on my own. I was Hawkeye. I could slouch a little in class. I could sit in the back row. I could make funny comments out the side of my mouth without being cracked on the back of the head with a yardstick. I was wise in the ways of unspoken social mores and I could move silently but confidently under cover of my new persona. My days of sitting stiffly on the front row of the Catholic Church were over. I enjoyed the freedom and embraced the responsibility.

The high elevation in the Rockies brings a wild swing of temperatures and seasons. Desert reds. Pine greens of winter. Snow that falls like powdered sugar. I felt at peace. But I had no interest in religion. God had mocked my birth and betrayed my childhood. I wasn't about to let Him play me like Odysseus. Any kind of public worship was a trap I avoided.

After two weeks I got a note to call home. My father wanted to talk to me. With a little trepidation I walked to the student union building and called him. He asked me two questions: *How are your studies going, and are you still on track to become a priest?* I wanted to say: *Gee dad, nice to talk to you. School here is real nice. I miss you too.* But of course I didn't. "My studies are going well," I answered.

Bill hung up the phone. Once again I had been dismissed.

CHAPTER

Eleven

*O*h, the freedom of college: a small room, a small bed. One small desk. A small lamp. There was no crucifix to condemn me. Nor would I be afraid to switch off the light at night. I went to the cafeteria and ate dinner alone. It was strange, being alone, no expectations. I couldn't tell if I liked it or not. One night I went outside the main residence door and stood out on the commons, looking up at the night sky. The stars were the brightest I had ever seen. I would later find high desert places to look at the stars. It made the Universe so real to me.

While staring up, I heard a voice from behind me. "Dark night, isn't it?" I turned around and saw a young man about my age staring up at the stars and smoking a cigarette. He said it was his first semester. I told him it was mine as well. We were two kids fresh out of high school connected by a common geography. He had a car, so we went for coffee. We pounded the syrupy black stuff with lots of cream and sugar the way teenagers do.

And we talked about our lives. We could not have been more different. I talked about my strict Catholic upbringing, being careful to not reveal too much. He talked about growing up in Las Vegas, sin city. He had memories of baseball and family outings and cousins who lived nearby. I talked a little about the beach then turned the conversation to cars. A deft social move. It was guy talk at its best. I could almost smell pipe tobacco. We kept the topics tangible: carburetors and road trips, nothing that would reveal feelings beyond romantic notions of adventure. Nothing real. That's how young men talk when they first meet. They find common ground on things that will not risk tipping a hand to vulnerability. I was a master at it, like Hawkeye, I had a lifetime of experience in the woods of masked emotions. I could sense where a trail was leading and gently push the conversation out of danger. We talked that way until 6am and then went our separate ways, having shared a campfire at the all-night diner.

I made friends easily in college. I even sponsored a Halloween toga party in my dorm room. The mix of students in the small college town were interesting. Athletes and farmers, kids from cities who wanted a small town experience. One friend was Jake. He was the first farm kid I ever met. Californians put on airs, that's just how the culture works. Jake was against any pretense. He wore overalls and had big hands and forearms from manual labor. I connected with him immediately because he delivered one-liners and was always happy. His drawl was infectious. I wanted to share things with him about my life, but masculinity forbade it. So we laughed a lot together and went off for pancakes between classes and he taught me about farm life. He loved it, third-generation.

But there was something different about him, more than the wholesome farm boy persona. I invited him for a beer and he declined. What twenty-two-year-old kid declines a beer? I jokingly said, "I won't tell your parents."

He smiled. He told me he had been a missionary for his church. I left it at that because I didn't want to get into a religious conversation. I mistrusted religious people but I really liked Jake. I was open to discussions about God, more from a metaphysical view, although I had life moments that make you scratch your head and wonder if something was going on behind the spiritual curtain. Again I was conflicted. Was God real or just an intellectual exercise? It was a classic argument for college kids emerging from under their parent's wings.

As a ten-year-old boy I learned scriptures in Catholic school that didn't jive with Catholic teachings, or at least that I couldn't understand. Close to our church in our neighborhood growing up were two other denominations, Jewish and Baptist. I was troubled by Jesus just being the Christ of Jerusalem. I wanted to know where he travelled and what he taught in the rest of the world and so I wandered over to the Synagogue. I didn't find the Rabbi, but there were some very kind people who explained to me that Jesus was a "nice man" and that if I wanted to know more about him I should ask my priest. I had tried asking the nuns to explain the trinity and got rapped on the knuckles. To me, every priest and Monsignor and Cardinal had it in for me and were just looking for a reason to cast me out onto the streets to be mocked by passersby. Having been traumatized already, my mind went to the worst possible scenarios. But I did venture over to the Baptists. Again, there I was met by the same story. A woman in a hat was being very patient with me, but not really answering the question. She told me to believe in Jesus, to accept Him, and that I would be OK in the end.

I think I was curious about other people's take on God because the God Ben and Bill represented was so punitive. The Baptists and the Jews gave me hope. Their kindness was uplifting. I watched them and they seemed genuinely concerned about each other. And their kids didn't seem to have as many rules as I did.

Outside of that first phone call, I didn't hear much from Bill and Helen after I arrived on campus. And I didn't know any Catholics in college. Monsignor Hawkes made it clear that he would continue paying the tab so long as I was on the path to the priesthood. I wasn't. And I wondered if my father would tell him. Being a priest was the last thing I wanted to become. Being religious at all conjured up images of a punitive God.

Not once in all my growing up life had I ever felt like I should serve God. I only felt I should fear Him. Jake smiled about his missionary service. He told me he loved it. It was the first time I realized that we could love God not just serve him as ministers of punitive judgment. This opened up a whole new set of feelings for me. And just in time.

But there was still Monsignor Hawkes. He called me from Los Angeles. "How are your grades?" He asked. I answered that I was doing fine. "I have a trip planned to Hawaii, would you like to come along?" This seemed out of the blue, and had to have some kind of motivation behind it, like hush money. Still, it was a trip to Hawaii. "Can I being a friend?" I asked. Surprisingly, Monsignor Hawkes agreed. So I invited a friend one of my apartment mates from the basketball team to an all-expense-paid trip to Hawaii at an exclusive resort.

We flew to Los Angeles. I stayed at the rectory in my old room and my friend stayed in another room. I tossed my bag in my room and waited for the Monsignor to finish up some paperwork. "You must be dirty from your flight," he said over his shoulder. "Go take a shower." I didn't move. "No thank you," I said. "I don't need a shower."

Monsignor Hawkes whipped his big leather chair around abruptly. He glared at me through those small eyes of his. "If you ever tell anyone, you're out!" There was an anger in his voice that frightened me. But I could tell he was losing his grip. Monsignor Hawkes had arranged a nice dinner for us at another ritzy restaurant, a place he could be seen feeding two young college kids. We had a nice meal. When we returned to the apartment at St. Basil's, I went into my room and left the light on and slept in my clothes.

The next day we flew to Honolulu. Accompanying us was a young man who was from South America who had also been an Altar Boy. The Monsignor had kindly invited him as well. That's when I knew the trip was about manipulation. Monsignor Hawkes was ever the showman, the perfect host. He entertained us with stories and we ate fine meals. It was all a façade, a way of building a case for his character in case accusations arose. The young man Monsignor Hawkes brought with him was still under the spell of the powerful priest. He was shy and very reserved. I tried to get him alone where we could talk but to no avail. Days were spent bodysurfing in the ocean and lounging on the beach. After another fine dinner, my friend and I rang up large room service and bar tab. We were there to have an enjoyable time, and we did.

On the morning we were to head to the airport, the Monsignor burst into our room to wake us up. He immediately jumped on my friend and began tickling him to wake him up. That in itself is strange behavior. We were college kids not 12-year-olds. My friend fought him off and finally Monsignor Hawkes left so we could get ready. While we were packing our bags the friend turned to me and said: "What's with your uncle? Is there something wrong with him? He grabbed my privates. That's just weird."

I was horrified, and terribly embarrassed. There was no conceivable way I could tell my friend that Monsignor Hawkes was a pedophile. Not only would he hate me for bringing him on this trip knowing that, but word would spread quickly and I would be ostracized. "Yea," I said, trying to brush it off. "That is weird." But inside I was furious.

We met the Monsignor, downstairs to checkout. He was looking at the bar tab we charged to the room he paid for. He grabbed me by the shirt collar and pulled me aside. "How dare you take advantage of the generosity I have shown you!" he said. His face was red with anger. I just stared back. The irony was thicker than the sticky Hawaiian air.

We boarded the plane and headed back to college. I regret not ever having a chance to talk to the young man from South America. Years later he had the courage to speak up, to be one of the accusers to add his name to the list sent to Cardinal Mahony outing Monsignor Hawkes as a pedophile. I admired him. I could have punched Monsignor Hawkes right there in the lobby of the Hawaiian hotel, but I didn't. I wished I had. But this kid came forward and told the truth no matter what happened to him; he spoke up.

I was a back row sitter in college. It was a habit I could not break. It was a good place to be if you wanted to keep the nuns in sight. I could also scan to determine who might be considered friend or foe. A few weeks into the semester, I noticed a particularly cute girl sitting in the front row. She seemed attentive and studious. No, that's a lie. She was attractive and carried herself with a lot of confidence. I would find out that she was studious later. In that first moment I was both enamored and nervous. It seemed to me that she might be the kind of girl who could read my soul, and I had too much to hide to take that chance. I kept her in my sights, at a distance.

The campus was crisscrossed with sidewalks across broad lawns that led to a mix of institutional-type buildings built on a budget, and the more classic architecture you would expect on a college campus. It was quaint and non-threatening. I walked between buildings a lot, enjoying the pleasant weather. That's when I spotted her again. She was walking with a friend. I believe in the luck of the Irish and I also believed I was clever enough to come up with an irresistible introduction. I failed miserably. "Hey, aren't you in my sociology class?" I asked. "I'm Mike. I'm from California. I'm a surfer." In the history of pickup lines, that is probably the lamest ever uttered.

The girl was more beautiful up close: petite, brunette. She was self-assured enough to smile and say something nice; I don't remember exactly what it was because I was trying to come up with something genuine, something that didn't make me come off as a player. I know she at least smiled. She seemed honest and was amused at my attempt at being cool. She didn't make me feel stupid and that made me want to get to know her even more. I had failed miserably at dating in high school. But pushing back against Bill and Monsignor Hawkes had given me a newfound courage.

I would try again.

The next time I saw her was in the Student Union Building. I had gone down to check my mailbox, only because I was bored. . And there she was, checking the mail in her box. I was prepared with a better line this time; actually it came out quite naturally. "I never get any letters!" I did over-dramatize it a bit, with a sorry tone. She smiled without looking at me.

The next day I had a letter from her that included her room number and phone number asking me to drop by and meet her and some of her friends. Now the dilemma: play it cool and drop by in a few days or wait a few hours and call that night. I did neither. I ran straight to her dorm. I'm not much for subtlety. I could irritate Bill by intentionally saying my Hail Marys too fast, or get kicked out of Catholic school for challenging religious teachings and being a nuisance.

I think I was sweating by the time I reached the girl's dorm. I had to calm myself, not be impulsive. This was a first meeting with a girl not from California. I could've turned up smelling like a brewery after some much-needed Dutch courage. But no, I wanted my wits about me.

She opened the door. Her name was Susan. She invited me in, made a joke about surfing or something, and we sat down to talk. This is the part where I can tell you that there is a God. And I don't say that lightly because up until then I had a vague sense of an angry being who ripped me out of my mother's arms, trafficked me to California to be abused and seemed to be done with me.

The truth was, I was just getting to know God. That first day with Susan was really the first day of understanding who I was. Susan asked me about my life. I told her I was a twin, adopted from Ireland.

"Sounds like Oliver Twist to me, right?" she asked.

The first sign you've just met your soul mate is that you both love Dickens, I reckoned then—and I still reckon it today.

"I know more about Oliver Twist than I do my own history," I said.

The nuns at the orphanage and my adoptive parents kept everything about me locked up tight. I had tried to pry info out of them. I even snuck into Bill's office when I was twelve-years-old, desperately looking for clues. The only answer I ever got was that I was "abandoned." This first meeting with Susan began my forty-year search for some real answers about the real me.

She was the first person I had ever told my adoption story to. Growing up nobody had ever asked, not friends or relatives. Something about Susan made me open up. I sat with her, hoping that my story ended the way Oliver Twist's did... with a happy family. I trusted her so completely, and so immediately, because she was so kind, so forthright. I had highly tuned antennae by then that could sense insincerity or feigned interest in order to gain advantage. Susan had none of that. There was nothing hiding beneath the softness of her countenance, only a fervent desire to know the truth. We became fast friends. She became the detective of my life as we both tried to discover the truth. It was thrilling to have someone so enthusiastic about uncovering your origins, your ancestors, the place you come from and the connections that were lost. She had all hope of reconnecting me to the web of relatives, for better or worse, she believed I deserved to know who I was.

More importantly, I was madly in love.

I've always been a big believer in serendipity; Susan had a very keen interest in genealogy and had been researching her own family roots for several years. She loved the nuts and bolts of the detective work and what it took to solve the mystery of a life story.

At the college mailbox that momentous day, I had received a letter, not from home, but from the woman who opened up my life and heart and brought me to a true sense of knowledge that there was decency in the world. I found somebody I could trust. We spent date nights talking about my mysterious Irish past and enjoying the mountains. Every date brought new revelations, and new closeness.

I ignored the notes that came from the student union to call home. I was happy and didn't want the weight of Bill's and Helen's piety slowing me down. What had always troubled me about my adoptive parents was that they never really sought God in the way seekers do. They were trapped in a kind of superficial religious caste system that valued appearance more than worship. I say this specifically about my parents, not about all Catholics. I had Catholic friends who earnestly tried to be good people and please God. But the power structure created by Monsignor Hawkes and his ilk demanded loyalty to their empire—a network similar to ancient city-states, government allegiances, and the spoils collected from innocent followers.

Then I made a mistake. I was so in love with Susan that I had to share it with Bill and Helen, and with Monsignor Hawkes. I wanted them to know that I was happy despite all their efforts to grind me into something less than human. I had found happiness. I wrote two letters, one to St. Basil's, and one to Bill and Helen. I told each that I was falling in love, how wonderful it felt, how much I looked forward to the future with Susan. The response from Bill and Helen was immediate. "We told you to keep to yourself, to focus on your studies. We told you NOT TO DATE!"

Monsignor Hawkes was even more direct. To him, I was still on the path to the priesthood, a place where he could always control me. Little did he know that I had left that path years ago lying in my bed at Priest camp. "Be mindful of your parents, your family, your obligation to Jesus Christ," he wrote tersely. I could almost see the same look on his face he gave me when I refused to take a shower. The trip to Hawaii was an attempt to keep a grip on me by showing me the wonderful material blessings of being a priest. This letter was purely a guilt trip. I kept the letter to remind me of what I was slowly separating myself from.

A few days later I was sitting in English class when a note was delivered to me from the office. "Call home." When class was over I went to the student office and dialed long distance. Might as well face it head on. True to his character, Bill had let things stew. His first blows across my backside were always reticent. But once he got going his anger took over and he really let me have it. He must've boiled for a couple days before picking up the phone and calling the student affairs office.

He made it clear that if I continued dating Susan I would be cut off from the family. Worse still, he threatened that I would lose my Catholic scholarship since I would no longer be considered a practicing Catholic! There was no mention of God in the conversation, only the "embarrassment," as he put it, to the family. Not being a priest was OK, but leaving the church dishonored the family!

I remember thinking to myself, "Gee, cut ties to the man who sexually abused me and stop having Christmas with the parents who belittled and beat me in favor of life with a woman who loves me and showed me God's love? Tough question."

"Fine," was my one word answer to Bill's threat.

He hung up immediately.

My father didn't take failure very well. I now wish he would have understood forgiveness better. But in his black and white world for me you either did as you were told or you were damned to hell. He knew his brother was a pedophile. I suspect he knew it when he was sending me there on weekends. He was loyal and did what was expected. In retrospect it caused him a lot of emotional pain.

Monsignor Hawkes' response was more melodramatic. He flew up from LA with one of his protégés in tow, a young man attending school at USC. We tried hard to find a nice restaurant to have the chat and ended up at a pizza joint. At dinner, Ben smiled at the young USC student, then lit into me. "You need to drop that girl and get out of here," he said in a way that felt like he was telling me to back the car up and go a different direction. "I will get you a full-ride to USC," he continued. "And we'll get you a car, a new one."

"A Mustang?" I asked.

Ben looked directly at me and nodded slightly.

I let the moment hang, then answered: "I don't think so. I'm staying."

I spent the whole night walking around the small town just to feel myself go any direction I wanted. I would even say out loud at times: I feel like going right, and I would make a quick turn and walk for an hour in that direction. It was a ritualistic night of making my own decisions. I was deliriously happy.

Susan and I were married in 1982. Neither Monsignor Hawkes, nor my older biological sisters attended the wedding. My parents, Bill and Helen Hawkes attended and were very congenial. My twin sister, now in the military, was stationed abroad and sent a note that curiously said she was glad that I had found happiness. I couldn't speak to her of the abuse at the hands of our uncle. I didn't want her to feel the weight of my pain. She was on her own journey away from the family. I guess the Hawkes had failed to save both our souls.

That same year, Ben Hawkes was listed in Los Angeles magazine as one of the most powerful men in LA. The Los Angeles Times referred to him as, "A legend."

CHAPTER

Twelve

In the mid 1980s while married to a wonderful woman, I found my thoughts and nightmares still drifting back to my early years. I thought often that I needed to visit Monsignor Hawkes. I wanted to confront him but I found it difficult to even consider the thought of seeing him. I couldn't see the rest of my life being haunted by the troubled emotions of my childhood. I wanted to slay the dragons and be done. I suppose I also wanted closure, or maybe I wanted Susan to meet him so I could open up a conversation with her about what he had done to me. But I lacked the fortitude. And then, on a trip to Disneyland, I found the courage and called him. He wanted to meet Susan and our new baby. My stomach tied itself up.

At that point in our life together, Susan didn't know the damage Ben had inflicted on me as an innocent young boy. That would be a later discussion. Susan felt it important to meet the Monsignor. I knew that she should, but I was apprehensive.

So, we traveled to Los Angeles to meet him. Our first child, Erin, was a few months old at the time. Ben invited us to dinner. Once again, I was summoned to St. Basil's church. It was so strange to step inside of that edifice haunted by dark emotions. Flashbacks of fear walking toward the sacristy troubled my thoughts. The great stone apostles seemed to be mocking me. Still, I wanted somehow to face and overcome the demons he had left me with. Entering St. Basil's I gripped Susan's hand. As an adult, I had no need to fear. I was even more physically imposing than he was.

My courage left me when he appeared. It was a dramatic entrance, out from the rectory and down the hallway, dressed in black like an angel of death. I became that small boy again. He shook my hand and smiled, seeing the secrets deep inside me that I kept from Susan. He touched Erin on the face and shook Susan's hand. For a moment I thought he was going to drag them both down to hell.

We went to dinner at one of Ben's favorite steak places, which was not too far from the church. It was expensive, of course. The meal cost more than a month's groceries for my little family. I was thankful for the food (and the doggie bag) but sweating in the presence of the man who was a demon. I was wedged between the essences of pure good and evil. On one side was the most important woman in my life. And on the other side was the very man who tried to destroy me. It felt as if there was going to be some grand choice between the two.

Ben noticed how difficult it was for us young parents to eat while holding a baby. He kindly offered to hold Erin while we ate. Susan relinquished and handed Erin to Ben. It was painful to see my firstborn in the arms of this monster. I had to tell Susan. I had to confront Ben, but I couldn't.

Monsignor Hawkes commented about Erin's comfortable place in his arms. Susan said to him, "Well, the contrast of black-and-white does help with a baby's visual development." As the priest was wearing a black suit with the white priest collar he quipped, "Well kids love me."

Monsignor Hawkes was charming. He was working hard to win Susan over. All I could see was the devil himself. He ordered desert and it was like he was taking her to Disneyland. I tried to refuse it, but he insisted. He sat back and smiled at me, almost daring me to say something here, in this refined place where he had many friends, here where he had won Susan over. "Go ahead, say something," he dared me with his look.

After leaving the restaurant, Monsignor Hawkes invited us back to the apartment at St. Basil's. "I have a gift for Susan," he said. So we took the short walk back to the soaring cathedral. Our footsteps echoed in the enormous space. His apartment was behind the rectory which included an opulent office. Luckily, Erin was getting fussy. Monsignor Hawkes entered the office, went behind his desk, opened a hand-carved wooden door on the credenza and drew out a box. Susan and I sat on the red couch in his office, the same red couch where I trembled in angst after he'd molested me in the sacristy. Flashes of torment and pain lit up my brain. I had suppressed the feelings until that moment when I felt the leather, smelled the office, smelled the same cologne when he bent down and opened the lid of the box and made an offering to Susan. The box was full of women's expensive jewelry. "Pick something," he said. "Something special."

Susan was sheepish, but picked out an emerald ring. She had no idea what it was worth, but I had seen such gifts delivered to Helen and the biological daughters. "Thank you," Susan demurred. We left quickly. Erin was ready for bed and playing her part perfectly.

We left the rectory of the church and I had failed. I wanted a confrontation and a win, I wanted to walk away feeling peace. I wanted Susan to know what I had been through. Instead, we had toured a grand church, had a steak dinner, and let Monsignor, the pedophile priest hold our baby. He had worked his way into our family with lavish gifts, paying for his sins. I had been revisited by the demons and didn't have the fortitude to face them. I cowered under their memory. I was still shackled by fear.

Eight years later we sold the emerald ring and bought a piano. It was blood money, a donation from some rich patron on her deathbed who expected to buy her way into Heaven. Instead of using it to feed the poor, the Monsignor used it to buy Susan's affection. I justified it by making sure our kids took piano lessons.

In 1985, Monsignor Hawkes submitted his resignation with the announcement of the newly appointed Archbishop, Roger Mahony. A few weeks later Monsignor Hawkes, at the age of 66 years, suffered a fatal stroke. Bill called me and was sobbing uncontrollably. I had never heard my father cry before. Susan sat beside me on our sofa, her hand clutching my arm and her head resting on my shoulder. Funny, I remember the smell of her hair and not how I felt, probably because I didn't feel anything. You would guess there would be a release, but there wasn't. Only Susan close to me.

"I would like you to be there," My father asked between sobs.

"Of course," I answered. "I'll be there." If I couldn't face him in life, I could at least condemn him in death.

I went to the funeral Mass alone. I didn't want Susan or our baby there. I met my family at St. Basil's hours before the service. We were ushered into Uncle Ben's apartment. It was me, the bastard child along with the chosen sisters and their parents. I expected there to be a reverent tribute to the late Monsignor, a few remembrances shared. I sat down on the red couch of hell and just watched. The family stood for a moment. The priest left us alone in the apartment. As soon as the door closed my father rifled through drawers looking for the will. Helen and the girls moved about searching for anything of worth. I sat dumbfounded. It was straight out of Dickens's Scrooge. They collected artwork and jewelry, and I half expected them to tear down the draperies for the fine cloth.

Then my father found the will. He looked over it while Helen and the sisters waited anxiously. Then Bill called me into The Monsignor's bedroom and closed the door. The bedroom, of all places. Uncle Ben had left me and my sister a little bit of money, a few thousand dollars. I was as surprised as Bill. But the look on Bill's face was one of anger. He looked me straight in the face as if he were about to tell me to go to my room and wait for him. Instead, he said: "This will be the last time a windfall will come your way."

I didn't want anything from that family meeting. Why would I want a reminder of the man who had molested me? For a moment I wanted to defy my father and deny the inheritance, but a few thousand dollars would help our little family so I took it.

Boxes were packed up from the office and we filed out, me empty-handed.

There was a lot of commotion outside St. Basil's. People lined up to get in and show off their devotions.

I stood with Bill and Helen and their two biological daughters. The crowd parted for the entourage of Archbishop Mahony. He approached us and expressed his condolences in a low monotone voice that felt as emotionless to me as the Latin chants.

My father knelt on one knee. The archbishop extended his hand and Bill kissed his ring. Helen wiped a tear from her eye, knelt and also kissed the ring. Each sister did the same. Then Archbishop Mahony was standing in front of me, his hand extended. I stood in front of him, my eyes looking directly at him. I reached my hand out and shook his. "Thanks for being here," I said. "Of course," he responded. "My sorrow is with the family."

The entourage moved slowly into the church; hundreds of priests and nuns followed by Hollywood's finest. We, his family, followed the casket to the front row. The enormous edifice that Monsignor Hawkes built filled up.

A letter from the Pope was read. The service was orchestrated in every detail to send the Monsignor to Heaven on incense and clothed in gilded robes. People wept openly and piously, mourners who needed a few more good marks in public. The elegy was for a man who had attained sainthood in this life. In an ironic twist, Monsignor Benjamin Hawkes oversaw "The Hawkes Home for Destitute Women" the year before he died. The name has since been changed to "The Good Shepherd Hawkes Residence," and shelters homeless women in Los Angeles.

When Archbishop Mahony took over as archbishop he severely limited Benjamin Hawkes financial responsibilities. He turned to the more underserved communities ignored by the previous archbishop and his powerbroker. Benjamin Hawkes was a symbol of excess. The poor needed to be served. But because he died shortly after the demotion, the Benjamin Hawkes legacy lived large within the upper LA circles. And his secret dark life seemingly died with him.

As I sat on the front pew with the Hawkes family, I thought: *No one knows this man. Is it even conceivable that I'm the only one who knows him?* Anger from time to time slipped in and out of my mind pondering my upbringing and relationships. As I sat thinking about the man being deified, my feelings and anger became more Intense. Emotions were finally coming to the surface.

As a boy, I had looked up to this man as a symbol of virtue. I was a boy desperate for acceptance and saw Benjamin Hawkes as a man of power, a member of God's inner-circle. I trusted him. My mind went back to the first time he abused me, how I had tried to brush it off as "normal," or as Ben's entitlement. I was so wrong to give him such sway, such room to be so lecherous and hypocritical. How could someone who had found a little boy, an innocent little boy who looked up to his uncle as such a strong figure—a religious backbone grounded in the Catholic hierarch— break the faith of trust that the little boy placed in him? I not only looked up to him as an uncle but also as a symbol of righteous arbitration who would wear the garments and robes of a priest. I could not in my early years think of him as anything less than an exemplar of sainthood.

In the drone of the Latin chants I heard the whispers of evil. I recognized it, finally. I knew then that I had been more than an abuse victim, I had actually been intentionally raised to be the priest's catamite. I had been in the stages of denial and fear for a long time, and now came the anger. It was all I could do to keep from shouting like a madman in the midst of the funeral.

I left the massive edifice and the largesse of the man who built it and flew home alone, shouting in my mind, shouting at myself. I shouted until the tears came and it was done, released. The scales fell from my eyes. I could finally talk to Susan.

I walked into our home exhausted. "I need to talk to you," I said. Susan turned to me, feeling that somehow I had to unburden myself. I gripped her hand. She collected the baby and we went for a drive. The road had always been the best way to unravel my emotions. We weaved our way along neighborhood streets, past small houses where families' lives were hidden from view. I let it all out. "Ben Hawkes is not who all those people think he is," I said. "He's a pedophile. He did horrible things to me, and to other boys."

Susan was horrified, but she had always suspected there was some kind of childhood trauma with the Monsignor. My anxiety around him gave me away. But she hadn't imagined how horrific the experience had been.

I had been raised on rote prayers and my mind was always abuzz with defense mechanisms, distractions, rationalizations, and the hum of angst. I needed to sort through it all with the only person in the world I could trust. I needed to pray, to really pray and pour out my emotions. I needed to know who God really was. I needed to know who I was and if I was salvageable.

We drove aimlessly for a time, then found a quiet park in Los Angeles. It was midday and the park was quiet. I remember the grass being well worn with large patches of dirt. Children had coursed the pathways from picnic tables to playground so often the grass had given up. Children. That's where my thoughts began. I had been a child. Nothing in my power could have prevented what had happened to me. Susan sat quietly holding Erin while I pondered, lifted the dark corners of my heart. It took some time to scrape the last remnants out, seeing each occasion of abuse from the priest, the physical and emotional abuse from my adoptive father. I had to examine each one and see how it shaped me, then discard the negative parts and keep the lessons learned. This kind of deep meditation takes time, and I'm sure my body language revealed the anguish and release I was going through.

Susan was patient and sat quietly. It is a process I would have to repeat a few more times with diminishing intensity until I was on more steady ground. But that first time was like a great and painful purging.

Ten years after Benjamin Hawkes died he would be cast aside like Harvey Weinstein and Jeffery Epstein. More accusers came forward. The headline of the LA Times article read: "Posthumous Fall From Grace." A letter arrived on Archbishop Roger Mahony's desk. That same LA Times that celebrated Benjamin Hawkes as one of the most powerful men in LA printed the contents of the letter: "It's my turn to stand up and set the record straight. Msgr. Hawkes was not a great priest, he was a sick man who used his status to abuse many." That letter was penned by one of his accusers, an altar boy I had stood next to in the sacristy in St. Basil's many years earlier.

I wish I'd had the courage to write the letter. I knew there were others. But I didn't have the strength to speak out.

About the time accusations were coming to light, I was invited to an annual memorial mass followed by a dinner gathering on the anniversary of the death of Monsignor Benjamin Hawkes. Nearly 100 people gathered every year. The after-mass gathering was hosted at the Hancock Park and Westside mansions Ben had frequented in life as he hobnobbed with the wealthy of Catholic Los Angeles society. To me, it seemed a gathering of perpetrators, enablers, and apologists—those who feared Ben Hawkes, even in death.

A brass plaque of him still hangs at St. Basil's. After all the negative press, the accusations, the settlements, the #MeToo movement, the Spotlight movie, it's still there—to me it seems a monument to power and perversion.

CHAPTER

Thirteen

he funeral, 10 years prior, put to rest, at least
somewhat, the monster Monsignor Hawkes. He
was no longer a physical threat, but he still haunted me
occasionally. Bill and Helen were alive and I felt a need
to stay connected. It was 1995; Susan and I were the
parents of Erin, age ten, Melissa age six and Christopher
age one. Susan had just gone back to college to complete
her Nursing degree. We were busy with work and kids'
activities. But I vowed to be the father that was always
there for my kids. We tag-teamed days that ended in
contented fatigue.

I found a classic Jaguar for sale and bought it. I put a lot
of work into it remembering my afternoons with Mr. Titus.

When it was finally tuned up and wiped down, I drove
the Jaguar up the coast to visit Bill. I wanted to prove to
him that I was doing just fine without him, the Catholic
Church, the Priesthood, the discipline of the rosary whip.

My need for a victory over my father drove me to this
act of vindication. Not very Christ-like. Bill came out and
I took him for a drive. We roared up the narrow roads

Mr. Titus and I had hijacked in my mind, taking over the territory in his chariot. I wanted Bill to feel what I felt, I wanted to say to him: this is what you missed with me when I was a boy. But we didn't talk.

When we pulled back into his driveway he touched the wood on the dashboard and without looking at me said: "You've done good for yourself, Michael." I've thought about that moment a lot. The more cynical part of me wants to think Bill was impressed by the car I was driving and measured me by that alone. But I also wonder if Bill was trying to apologize for everything he put me through, that the wind did him good and that he was happy I had somehow survived Monsignor Hawkes' abuse and not become a drunk embarrassment to the family. Susan thinks it was Bill's way of finally accepting me for who I am. Maybe.

Much of our genealogical sleuth work early on had reached dead ends. And having a family limited the time we could devote to it. But kids have a way with their parents, asking questions, wondering about grandparents. We didn't have a lot of great answers for them on my side, except that I was from Ireland. I told them fantastical stories about knights and High Kings in castles on far away mythical lands. Truth is, I knew little of Ireland except for what I read. It left me with a deep longing to know. There is a famous Irish tale about the Fish of all Knowledge. In that tale there is a promise that whoever eats the fish becomes the wisest man in all of Ireland. It felt a bit like we were fishing for that one thing that would answer all of our questions, one fish of all knowledge. But the answers would come in small bits as we cast about while the kids were sleeping.

Two letters were sent to the address and institution listed on my orphanage medical records from 1961, inquiring about my adoption and family details. But they went unanswered, "More dead ends. I figure it's just messy record keeping, or no record keeping," I told Susan.

Susan wanted to know about my family health history so we could be prepared for anything that might afflict the kids. That's how nurses think. They see nasty diseases all day and want to be prepared if something is coming their way. So we got back to work. In late 1996, while wrapping up her studies to become a registered nurse, Susan was expecting—this time with twins! We were all extremely excited. Especially me.

My twin sister was then the mother of 10-year-old twin daughters. Although she lived abroad, we had become closer as memories of childhood trauma were displaced by the current joys of raising children of our own. Now I would be the father of twin sons!

Two days before Thanksgiving Nicholas and Ryan joined the family six weeks early and came home on Thanksgiving Day. The older children were with Susan's parents. While we were driving the twins home I looked in the rearview mirror. "Twins, like me and my sister," I mused. I think that's the moment when I really felt my mother's heartache at giving us away.

Erin and Melissa, now ages 12 and 8, would wake early each morning to help with the babies before leaving for school. The small house was always abuzz. The family had never been happier. To have five children, a successful career and a future that included dreams of children growing up without heartache seemed ethereal.

I went with Susan and the babies to the pediatrician for their two-week well-baby checkup. The little boys were passing all the preliminary checks with flying colors—but then Nicholas' heart was checked with a stethoscope. The physician determined that he had a heart murmur. Our own hearts were now in our mouths.

We left there with an appointment for the following morning with a pediatric cardiologist. Driving away from the pediatrician's office, I looked again in the rearview mirror as Susan sat between the precious little sons, holding their tiny hands with tears streaming down her cheeks. It was as if she already knew.

The next morning, Nicholas was sedated prior to an echocardiogram in the cardiologist's procedure room. When the test was over, we sat nervously in the office of the physician and he began sharing the gravity of the complex cardiac congenital defects found during Nicholas' test. Just as the cardiologist explained, "You shouldn't be worrying that Nicholas will die suddenly; but he will need several heart surgeries in order to have adequate cardiac function."

Susan holding Nicholas, noted that he looked dusky, compared to Ryan who was sleeping in his carrier. She alerted the physician. The cardiologist checked Nicholas for a pulse—it was slow, above 100 beats per minute, but Nicholas was not breathing. The Physician immediately began giving Nicholas mouth-to-mouth rescue breaths.

Nicholas pinked up, was placed on Oxygen with a tiny mask, and hooked to a pulse oximeter, which read 39—a number forever etched in the soon to be Nurse mother's psyche.

With cardiologist in tow, we jumped in our minivan and drove across the street to the regional center, where the babies had been born, to have Nicholas admitted to the Neonatal Intensive Care Unit. We anxiously spent the next four days alternating time at Nicholas' bedside, staring at the heart monitor. We were informed in days to come that Nicholas was deteriorating and would need surgery.

Susan's parents, who had been in town for the births but since gone home, immediately returned to help with the older children. Nicholas was transferred to Children's Hospital Los Angles for surgery. He went through the surgery on December 18th and per the pediatric cardiothoracic surgeons, did especially well. Susan and I stayed by his crib until late that evening. Nicholas was stable and still under post-operative sedation. We were exhausted and went home to tiny Ryan and the older children to get some sleep. It was restless at best.

The phone rang at 1:30 AM. I sat up in bed, hoping it was the alarm. We both rushed to answer. The quivering voice of the physician on the phone said, "Nicholas has taken a turn for the worse. How fast can you get here?"

Prior to calling us, the attending physician had inadvertently called the emergency contact number Susan had listed; the number of a dear friend of the family, Gary. He was already on our front steps as Susan and I were rushing out the door. Gary offered kindly to follow us to the hospital. Susan's parents arrived from their nearby hotel to be home with the sleeping children. In the rush of emotions images of a punitive God resurfaced. It couldn't be true that He was going to take our baby away from us.

We drove to the hospital in horrified silence. On arrival a young physician, eyes wide with trepidation, led us to a waiting room, explaining that Nicholas had gone into cardiac arrest, and they had been performing CPR for nearly an hour.

We each prayed silently that this precious little child would be able to come home to his family. Twenty agonizing minutes ticked by. I prayed to God, pleading for the life of my son.

The cardiothoracic surgeon and cardiologist walked into the room. The look on their faces said it all. The resuscitation efforts had failed. Nicholas was gone. How do you survive this grief, the loss of a baby? How do you go home and tell your sweet children that their beloved little brother is dead? How do you explain that God did not answer this prayer? How do you live with some normalcy when you have to un-twin?

I had planned a life that included all of our children. Now, one was gone. I think in that time I felt the separation from my sister more acutely. I longed to be comforted by my own flesh and blood. But she was a world away. Susan had been *my everything* since our first date. She filled the holes in my soul perfectly until this raw wound opened up. Susan had supported me in life, and I her. this was a new moment of fear and we leaned on each other.

The drapes of Nicholas' room in the cardiothoracic pediatric ICU were closed for privacy. Susan and I, along with our dear friend Gary were escorted into the room. Nicholas' tiny body, dressed and swaddled, was handed to Susan. The room was very quiet and peaceful. No words were spoken. Tears were streaming but silent.

Susan said, in a soft, trembling voice, "I'll never be able to hold him again."

Gary, a bereaved father himself, who had experienced his precious infant daughter's death 15 years prior, said quietly but surely, "Yes you will. I know this is not the end."

"I know, but in this life . . . this is too final," Susan said softly, barely able to speak.

It must've been difficult for Gary to be there. It was the same hospital in which his daughter died, also of a congenital heart defect. Gary slipped out of the room and called Susan's parents.

My spiritual senses had changed dramatically since marrying Susan. God was loving. God was kind. God had a plan. Still, the ghosts of a mocking God shook me.

Hours later, as the sun was coming up, we drove home in silent, abject grief. The hardest thing Susan and I have ever had to do was tell the children about their brother's death. I fell into a crisis of faith. Since leaving home I had been happy. I had wonderful children. It seemed I had stepped out of the dark into the light, and when this new darkness fell I could not understand why.

The service for little Nicholas was held on December 23rd. How do you bury your child the day before Christmas Eve? It was so difficult to go through this during the holiday season, especially with our children, at a time of year that is about bringing joy and hope into the home. Friends and family gathered around us with their thoughts, prayers, and needed hugs. Wonderful family members on Susan's side and dear friends from the neighborhood, work colleagues, professors, and nursing students, and many of my work associates passed by the little white casket. People we loved wept with us and expressed sincere sadness and condolences.

A scripture I had learned came to mind and gave me a glimpse of peace: "Are not two sparrows sold for a farthing? And one of them shall not fall on the ground without your Father." [Matthew 10:29, KJV] Two sparrows, neither unnoticed by God.

Because our thoughts were with Nicholas' struggles, we had not prepared an entirely proper Christmas for the other children. We had tried; did some hurried shopping on Christmas Eve, but the tree seemed a little bare, almost painful to even look at.

The phone rang. It was Gary. He said, "Michael, a few friends have put together a Christmas for Erin, Melissa, Christopher, Ryan, Susan and you."

At first my reaction was to not want to be on the receiving end of people's benevolence. I was still trying to pull myself out of self-pity. But as our little grief-stricken family sat at home on Christmas Eve, there was a quiet knock on the door. Dear friends delivered beautifully wrapped gifts and placed them underneath the little Christmas tree. A part of our broken hearts was mended. "This was God," I thought. "To be with those who mourn." Who else but a benevolent maker could rescue us from our grief with the love he imparted to good friends who were so willing to share that love with us.

Almost as quickly as my faith crisis began, it was dissipating. My understanding of God was moving out of the confusion of a traumatic childhood to one of confidence in a benevolent, perfect love no matter the difficulties of life. I remembered a line from Finnegan's Wake: *He is cured by faith who is sick of fate.*

A COLLECTION
OF MEMORIES

**Michael and the Reverend Mother at Black Rock
Temple Hill Orphanage.**

Michael and the Reverend Mother.

Michael's passport on his way to the U.S.

Reverend Msgr. Hawkes with Michael at age 7

Elizabeth "Betty", Michael's mother.

The Cleary family, 1921.

Tony, Susan, Maura and Michael, Dublin 2014.

Michael and Susan at the door where I last saw my mother.

Michael's biological father, Patrick Ryan.

**Barney Ryan (Michaels brother), Anne Ryan,
Michael and Susan.**

John Ryan, Michael, Barney and Annette.

At O'Sheas the Ryan family pub with Kevin, Lee and Ben.

Michael and Susan, Dublin 2015.

Christopher, Erin, Melissa and Ryan. Michael and
Susan's children, London.

Hawkes children and grandchildren at Betty's grave.

Barney and Michael in deep conversation about family history,
Bray, Ireland.

CHAPTER

Fourteen

The death of our baby left us heartbroken yet focused on the things that matter most; family, faith, and love for one another. We had to learn to live as a bereaved family. Parenting and work obligations filled up our days and nights.

In 1996, prior to the upheavals of births and death in the family, the LA Times featured an article about previous decades of forced and potentially nefarious adoptions from Ireland. The article listed a hotline number that could be called to inquire about details; if you had been an Irish child adopted to the USA. I called the number that week. We were informed that St. Patrick's Guild was the organization who arranged the adoption and held my records.

The loss of Nicholas had further turned my heart toward an urgency to find my birth mother. She, after all, had lost two babies. Eventually we began to emerge from the fog of grief and could concentrate on continuing the hunt for truth of my early life.

Before finding the name of the adoption agency, I only had my Irish passport from 1961, the names of my natural parents, as listed on my original London birth certificate, and immunization and medical records from Dublin that had been sent with me at the time of the adoption. Helen and Bill had given the documents to me when I was about to marry. It was an interesting exchange. It was a cutting of the strings. "You may as well have these," was the cold note's punch line. No affection.

Letters were sent to procure an official copy of my birth certificate and baptismal certificate from London. I sent the following to Sister Gabriel, St. Patrick's Guild, 82 Haddington Rd., Dublin 4, dated 21 February 1997:

Dear Sister Gabriel,

My name is Michael Anthony Hawkes. I spent the early years of my life in Ireland and was adopted by an American family in 1961. I was given your name and address in response to my phone call to a number published in the Los Angeles Times newspaper regarding children who were adopted in Ireland and sent to American families. I have copies of my medical history and vaccinations from 1961 prior to my adoption (copy enclosed) from St. Patrick's Infant Dietetic Hospital, Temple Hill, Blackrock Co., Dublin. I was told that I spent my first 3 years of life at this facility. My passport from 1961 states that I was a citizen of Ireland at the time. My passport was issued July 19, 1961, and I was admitted to the United States in New York on July 28, 1961. I have been told by my adoptive parents that my original name was Michael Anthony Mancell and that my biological parents' names were Patrick Mancell and Elizabeth Esther Cleary...

I went on to give each detail that I had and asked for help in procuring more documents and information about my mother and biological family. This was in the midst of a groundswell of inquisitions and letters to government representatives. I wasn't the only Irish baby sent abroad under suspicious circumstances, and denied access to public records. Six weeks after I sent the above letter, during the Dail Eireann debates to the National Parliament in Dublin, on 9 April 1997, politician Alan Shatter delivered the following impassioned speech:

Thank you, Sir, for letting me raise the need for an adoption contact register. It is unacceptable that an adoption society such as St. Patrick's Guild has deliberately misled people by giving grossly inaccurate information, both to adopted persons and to birth mothers, with regard to the background to their adoption. It is almost beyond belief that an adoption society deliberately set out to tell adopted persons the wrong names, wrong dates of birth and the wrong ages of the birth mothers. That behavior must be totally condemned by Members of this House.

It is an extraordinary indictment of the lack of humanity shown to persons with a genuine need for information about their background that they were subjected to such conduct. I say that as someone who is well aware of the good work our adoption agencies have done over the years and the great deal of care many agencies, including this agency, have shown over the years with regard to

adoption placements and ensuring families with
whom children were placed were suitable.

It is simply unacceptable that the events which
have now come into the public arena occurred. I
ask the Minister to ensure that the behavior of this
adoption society is rectified and to seek assurances
from that society that it maintains accurate records
that can be utilized in circumstances where both
adopted persons and birth mothers are trying to
establish contact with each other.

Nothing changed.

On 28 April 1997 I received a letter from St Patrick's Guild. They had received my February 1997 letter of enquiry. Sister Francis Ignatius was now assigned to my case. She listed in the letter, along with a few confirming details and misleading data points, that Saint Patrick's Guild had indeed been the adopting body in 1961. She also stated, "In recent years we have had many requests similar to your own and we now have a waiting list before we can begin to do any tracing."

Several phone calls to St Patrick's Guild were made in the next eleven months, and the answer was always the same, "You are in the queue. We will get to you in turn." Years later I would meet Martin Sixsmith, the man who brought the story of Philomena to light. I made a short appearance in a BBC documentary about Ireland's Lost Babies. We had a little time to chat. "I'm not surprised at the resistance you ran into," he said. "Their tactics are to stall, misdirect, and deny."

At first, I gave them the benefit of the doubt. Austere elderly nuns with bad memories and sloppy record keeping.

In the Philomena story the adoption facilitating entities claimed that fire had burned years' worth of records. Looking back I can see their tactics as clearly as Martin Sixsmith described. But at the time, I was just uncovering the deceit.

A letter from Christine Gregory, Social Worker from St. Patrick's Guild, dated 7th April 1998, nearly one year later read:

Dear Mr. Hawkes,

I hope this letter finds you and your family well. Sr. Francis wrote to you in April 1997 explaining that due to the numbers of tracing requests we were receiving that unfortunately we had to compile a waiting list. As such your request came then to my attention.

Mr. Hawkes, I located your birth mother's address and wrote to her in January of this year. Without disclosing the full details of my enquiry, I asked that she contact me. When I did not hear from her immediately, I did not worry unduly as quite often it does take birth mothers time to recover from the surprise of being contacted after so many years.

Having waited what, I felt was an appropriate period of time I rang your birth mother's home, where upon I spoke to her sister. Unfortunately, Mr. Hawkes your mother had been very ill for a considerable time, and sadly she passed away in October of last year.

Bollocks!

The letter continued, as did subsequent letters, to discourage further searching. Christine Gregory stated that their records indicated that only Elizabeth's mother had been aware of the pregnancy and births. Also stated was that I should be aware that living family may not be receptive to communication. They would use every tactic to try to dissuade my continued search, even gas lighting.

Still grieving the loss of Nicholas and now my birth mother and needing to concentrate on healing myself and family, I dropped the search. I was not ready for additional grief and rejection. I did however ask Christine Gregory to send a copy of my mother's death certificate, which she had offered. It was never sent.

For a time, I turned to my own small family for joy and connection. These were happy years. I had vowed to give my children the love and attention they deserved. Susan taught me how.

CHAPTER

Fifteen

*I*n 2005, I had the opportunity to collaborate with several individuals who remained in positions within the archdiocese of Los Angeles. They were clients of the company I worked for. They paid us well. They called me and asked me to create some graphic design for some of their humanitarian efforts. I took the job as we were always welcoming new clients. I also believed that there were some good people in the Catholic Church, and I wanted to find them.

Prior to one of my meetings, a top ranking monsignor of the Los Angeles archdiocese, approached me, with a stricken look on his face, telling me that he urgently needed to speak to me.

I began to feel a bit of anxiety as he briskly ushered me to the Cardinal's conference room. The monsignor then proceeded to tell me that a class action lawsuit had been filed by victims accusing the archdiocese of covering up years of systemic clerical sexual abuse by priests within the archdiocese. A judge had ruled that the names of those priests could be made public.

With tears in his eyes, he informed me, "I am the bearer of very sad news. Your uncle, Monsignor Ben Hawkes, has been named as an abuser by two former altar boys at St. Basil's. He was accused of being implicated in the systematic protection of pedophiles by facilitating their movement."

I was not moved at all. The news was no surprise. The lack of emotion in my response must have been confusing to him. He was in tears, and I was indifferent. I had come through life with this curse around my neck. It didn't matter to me what the LA Times printed. In fact, it was about time. The monsignor then went on to express his opinion that the alleged victims were simply "weak people."

I stood up, shook his hand and he said, I need to ask you one thing. Will you call your father and tell him as soon as possible.

I knew exactly who the two altar boys were. I had served mass with them many times as twelve-year-old boys. I could recall their faces in horror as we stood shoulder to shoulder in the sacristy ready to serve mass, but instead were groped by the infamous and still highly regarded Monsignor Hawkes. What strikes me now is that he would molest us all, in front of the others, a lecherous monster feeding on the purity of children. Like the mythological monster Lamia, who feasted on her own offspring, these priests groomed children and young men to satisfy their own lusts.

These two grown accusers of Monsignor Hawkes had been young vulnerable kids, in precarious positions, beholden to Ben Hawkes' good graces, just as I had been. I hadn't seen them in years. I was heartbroken for the other boys, now adults. I hoped their journeys were less painful than mine.

I suddenly had the daunting task of calling my father, the older brother of the late Monsignor, and telling him that this legend of a priest had another very dark side and was not a legend but a serial abuser of young innocents. His brother was a man charged with protecting those who could not protect themselves but instead took his position as pastor and leading prelate to satisfy his lusts.

I should have been elated. The truth had come out yet it was nothing more than a tragedy.

I found a quiet place in the house and called my father. "Dad, it's Michael" I began.

He was older, and his voice not as commanding as it was in my growing up years. "Hello Michael. How are you and the family?"

"They are well, thank you." The small talk was over quickly. "I have to tell you something, dad," I continued. "I was called to the Cardinal's office today. It was urgent."

Silence on the other end.

"Your brother was named in a lawsuit and is accused of having abused children; that served as altar boys from his parish."

I opened my mouth to say the words: *and I too was his victim as a child.* But I couldn't. Bill was an elderly man by then and I thought the news I bore was heavy enough. "The two boys were at St. Basil's the same time I was there, serving mass."

Still, my father was silent.

"Dad, an article will soon appear in the Los Angeles Times, the front page."

Bill broke his silence. "Thanks for telling me, Michael," and hung up the phone.

Where was the shock, the outrage at the accusation, the denial? When Ben decided on a path to the priesthood, his mother was overjoyed. Having a priest son rubberstamps your passport into Heaven. Ben became the golden boy and Bill the son that would always be less-than. I'm sure much of Bill's frustration was taken out on the children he never wanted. We were thrust on him by his brother and Bill, bound to some saintly expectation, agreed to it. But every upsize in Ben's career diminished Bill. He wasn't given to self-flagellation, but he wasn't above taking the belt to the two little Irish kids.

In October 2021, *The Guardian* reported that as many as 3,200 French Catholic priests had been pedophiles since 1951. That's in France alone. No numbers yet on America. My ability to process the emotions of how many victims that multiplies out to is impossible. I only knew the boys next to me who stood frozen in fear, eyes heavenward waiting for it to end, for someone to come to their rescue. And there was the young man in Hawaii I couldn't save. The light on their perpetrators, and those who transferred pedophiles to different parishes to hide their acts, was long overdue.

It was more than abuse. The Right Reverend Benjamin Hawkes, the Vicar General had been the archdiocese official responsible for moving sexual predators out of LA, to places like New Mexico. He blessed the souls of priests, forgave them, and shipped them off to new and fertile grounds to abuse again. The victims were shunned as "weak souls" who deserved their station in life. It seemed to me that every machination in the Catholic Church would be used to conceal the dark system of trafficking, abuse, molestation, and preservation of the system itself.

When Larry Nassar was being tried for molesting members of the women's gymnastics team, McKayla Skinner, one of the victims said something universally true of this kind of organization: "I feel like I'm fighting against a whole system, not just one man." My sentiments exactly.

In 2015, Pope Francis visited the United States. It was at the height of abuse accusations and many were calling for change in accountability of the priests. Victims were demanding meetings with the Pope. Journalists wanted to know why accused abusers were still serving in the church. Could this be a turning point in the Catholic Church?

We, the abused, were left sorely disappointed. Pope Francis expressed sorrow for the victims and at a special meeting for Bishops praised them for their courage and told them he felt *their* pain. It was clear where the Pope's heart was: with the priests. In 1986, the Priest Peter Hullerman was transferred from Munich to Essen because he had been accused of abusing an 11-year-old boy. He went on to abuse more boys and was convicted of pedophilia and distributing pornography. He served an 18-month sentence and then was reassigned where he worked another 20 years in close contact with children.

Many victims were angered by the light touch on the matter by the Pope. Victims wanted justice, the kind of justice that opens the doors to mercy and healing. What they got was the Pope denying he was even at the meeting that recommended transferring Hullerman, and Pope Francis appeal to forgive the offending priests. No recrimination of the priests. No solidarity with the victims. Only deflection of moral responsibility.

I made an appointment to meet privately with Cardinal Roger Mahony. Family ties got me in quickly.

I approached the office and the Heavy door opened up. Cardinal Mahony welcomed me in. The windows from this top floor of the building had a grand view of the Los Angeles cityscape. He seemed a gentle old man. We sat on chairs across from each other.

After polite greetings, I said to the Cardinal, "Cardinal, I know there have been public allegations against archdiocese priests, including my uncle." He responded, Yes Michael, I am very aware of the accusations.

"Cardinal, I have come here to let you know that the two gentlemen that accused my uncle need to be taken seriously."

He cocked his head to one side, surprised at my boldness. "And why is that?" he asked.

"Because," I told him flatly, "I was also a child victim of Monsignor Hawkes at St. Basil's church in the rectory and sacristy.

The old Cardinal suddenly turned from family friend to protector of the Catholic Church. "I'm sorry to hear that Michael," he said, looking away from me at the many photos he had on his wall of popes past and present. "I will keep you in my prayers."

We stood up, shook hands, and I left the office.

CHAPTER

Sixteen

In December of 2009 one evening my phone rang. It was one of the older sisters on the other end.

"Michael, I just wanted to let you know that Mom passed away earlier today."

My first words that just came out were: "I'm sorry."

I think I was saying to my sister that I was sorry that her mother had passed. It struck me as an odd feeling to say to a sister, "I'm sorry that your mother had just died."

But it was a genuine from my gut statement. "Is there anything you need?" I said. "How is Dad? She shared that our father was very quiet and deeply in mourning.

Plans were made for the body to be transferred to the family plot at a Catholic cemetery in the Los Angeles area. My father called me to ask if I could meet the mortuary van driver bringing my mother's body down from Northern California. I did. My wife and I met the van at the grave. A grave site that was a pre-planned Hawkes family plot for a father, a mother, grandparents, who died before my adoption, a priest uncle and 2 biological daughters. No room in the family plot for 2 adopted children.

A memorial service was planned a few weeks after the burial. Susan, our children, and I drove up to the church for the mass. My twin sister attended as well. The two older sisters spoke, as did I. It was pleasant enough. After there was a luncheon. It seemed cold and distant. I do not remember any tears being shed. No tears for a mother who tried. As she would say in life from time to time, "We did the best we knew how."

After we got in the car and drove back to Los Angeles.

In 2013, we contacted St. Patrick's Guild to pick up where our last search attempt had left off. It had been 18 years with no answers. The kids were mostly grown,

Correspondence wasn't working so we figured we'd knock on a few doors. The last correspondence from the Saint Patrick's Guild social worker was an offer to send the death certificate of Elizabeth Esther Cleary and follow up on a lead for my biological father. None had materialized in the last 15 years. I had my mother's and father's names as listed on my birth certificate. I had my original baptismal certificate from London. In the margins of the copy of the baptismal certificate, in script handwriting, it read, "Should anyone inquire about this document, contact William Hawkes (with his California address listed) immediately." My father—Bill—never mentioned to me that he had been notified. The 1998 nuns / social workers at St. Patrick's Guild had furnished none of the facts we had discovered. The Irish government was even less helpful. They simply said all records were with The Sisters of Charity for my Kilkenny years and with St. Patrick's Guild for the few months I was at Blackrock Temple Hill. How a government can skirt responsibility for so many years is hard to understand. They simply turned the process over to the Catholic Church. They paid the church entities to warehouse us without vetting or oversight. I think the government officials were glad to be rid of the whole mess—the expense of vetting families, creating an underclass of people who would be a drain on the dole.

The Irish playwright and novelist Mannix Flynn, who was sent to an industrial home at age 10 and suffered sexual and physical abuse there has this to say about Irish treatment of the poor: "The state saw us as surplus to needs. The British were relatively progressive when it came to the Poor Laws and orphanages and so on. I am not saying they were magnificent. But we went the other way. We were seen as undesirable. We were surplus to need. We couldn't possibly be intelligent. And where you had opportunity to put us away you could put us in the employ of the church."

I was part of the great undesirable population. Bureaucrats found an ideal solution. Let the Catholic Church take care of it, ship most of us unwanted babies away.

I contacted Saint Patrick's Guild, sending copies of all written correspondence to and from their office that had occurred since 1995. After initially being told they had no record of previous correspondence, I cited the 1998 document telling me that my mother was dead. They backtracked. I was then told that I would have to re-establish my request for information and to send copies of all prior correspondence, and proof of identification. They also made sure to tell me that there was a long waiting list. I explained that I was traveling to Ireland in six months time and wanted to find all we could before the trip. I was told that I was in the queue.

My sense is that enough light had been shed on the improprieties of the Catholic adoption system, the scandals of pedophile priests, and the Irish Government's offloading of responsibility had made top officials in every related church and state organization careful to cover their ignominious past.

Susan and I kept good humor about the whole thing, it was the only way we could keep pushing through it. I called the whole affair "The Immaculate Rejection" since everyone seemed to be clean of any wrongdoing.

Still, I had a history. My first three years were a mystery. Family connections were a completely unknown. There is a risk to finding out where you come from and who you are related to. In the end, I simply wanted to know. The truth was more important to me than a Pollyanna ending. I had to see it with my own eyes.

We had the original London birth certificate with birth parent names and the baptismal record we had received years before. The 2013 Internet was much more robust than it had been in 1998. We began with a search of St. Joseph's home in Kilkenny, St. Patrick's Guild and St. Patrick's, Blackrock Temple Hill.

The search for St. Josephs first resulted in a 54-page document on the Irish website childabusecommission.ie. St. Joseph's Industrial School, run by the Sisters of Charity, was one in which child abuse had occurred, as documented by now Dublin City Councilor Mannix Flynn. It also appeared to be a home for only girls during the time that Saint Patrick's Guild stated that I was there. Add that to the growing list of misrepresentations. Another Internet search uncovered a 2016 news story from the Kilkenny People newspaper with its headline, "Nuns Hid Abuse at St. Joseph's for 50 Years."

The mother load find of the Internet search came with the search for St. Patrick's Blackrock Temple Hill. This search resulted in finding the Internet site adoptionrightsalliance.com. Here was a group of individuals who had their own Irish adoption experiences and had been advocating for years for people like me. The members of the Adoption Rights Alliance (ARA) understood the runaround I had received from St. Patrick's Guild. They had been in the same labyrinth for years. It was as if I found a secret tribe searching for the same answers. We shared clues.

Finding the ARA website led to a link to the ARA Facebook page and the term "Banished Babies" What a term. That led to getting Mike Milotte's book, "Banished Babies; The Secret History of Ireland's Baby Export Business."

We were shocked to find such a history. We also discovered and read the book, Philomena, and later watched the movie based on the book. The parallels in the life of adoptee Anthony Lee, the son taken in Ireland from Philomena Lee, and sent to the USA, were heartbreaking.

The treatment of Philomena by the nuns, the anguish of separation, the difficulties of the adopted home, the deceit of those who intentionally kept Philomena and Anthony apart. Too many parallels; some of which we had not even yet discovered. We attended the opening show of the limited release of Philomena at a Hollywood, California theater. We walked out of the theater grief stricken. I had been diagnosed a few years earlier as diabetic and had a blood sugar drop from the emotional toll. I pulled the minivan over and Susan ran to a convenience store to get me a sugary soda. I remember feeling helpless. Although I had received a sense of calm and peace in my own theophany, the body is not immortal. Emotions trigger physical responses. Susan drove home while I felt the weight of so many banished babies.

The next day we contacted one of the founders of Adoption Rights Alliance (ARA). She also had been adopted as a toddler from Ireland to the United States. She and other ARA founders had devoted years of work toward advocating for Irish adoptees and Irish first mothers. Their advocacy has been, and continues to be, phenomenal. This ARA adoptee kindly referred us to a researcher, also an Irish adoptee, but one who had remained in Ireland. Her search expertise and support would change the trajectory of our pursuit.

We began connecting dots. Susan kept a chart with lines connecting dates, organizations, persons, and events. Friends joked that it looked like we were investigating a murder mystery. The more answers we found, the more questions we had.

On 25 November 2013 we contacted The ARA researcher and shared everything we knew from the birth records and information received from Saint Patrick's Guild regarding Elizabeth's death in 1998. Within a few days, the researcher went to the General Records Office (GRO) in Dublin and procured copies of Elizabeth Mancell (nee Cleary's) death certificate from Oct 1997, listing her daughter Eilish Mancell, with an address.

These were heady days. I could hardly wait to get home from work and sit with Susan, pouring through new discoveries.—The researcher, now our search angel (SA), an intrepid investigator was on the case! We have opted to leave her as anonymous to respect her privacy. She and Susan began corresponding on Facebook messenger.

The SA found the marriage information of my birth mother Elizabeth Cleary and her husband James and his 2003 death record from Wales. She found Eilish's birth certificate.

On Ancestry.com Susan found James in several trees, but with no addition of a wife or daughter. Susan sent a message on Ancestry to the tree owner, a great niece of James and got a reply that his niece was not aware that her great uncle had been married. Email correspondence with Sister Edith of Saint Patrick's Guild continued.

The SA, brilliant detective that she was, suggested that we tell Sister Edith that we had found biological relatives of James and were doing DNA tests to prove that the adoptions were illegal. A brilliant and sly move, but one that we figured could provoke the truth.

The SA also began searching the parish records from the last known (1998) address of Eilish and discovered that the house had been sold in 2012. On November 30, a message came from the SA: "Hi Susan, I rang Mount Argus parish as I found a death notice on their site for an Eilish Mancell Jan 2012. I got into a lovely woman in the office and I'm sorry to say Elizabeth / Eilish Mancell died last year."

Eilish had been hit by a car, while walking her dog; the SA ascertained from her conversation with the parish office.

Eilish had never married, had no children and had been her mother's lifelong companion. We were heartsick. We had missed finding Eilish by less than two years. The SA learned from the parish that Eilish and her dog Jackie, were village and parish fixtures; Eilish was loved by many.

The SA was told that Eilish was buried at Mount Jerome Cemetery. The dear and sweet SA generously asked if she could lay a Christmas wreath at the grave. She also found Eilish's death certificate. The certificate listed an informant, a cousin, Mr. Thomas Anthony Beatty—with an address.

As these pieces of the jigsaw came together, we began making a list of places in Ireland where we could gather evidence. There was so much to make sense of. Facts put you on the trail, but don't give you a sense of the feelings one must've been having at the time. We needed to find relatives and collect their stories. I would start with the cousin, Thomas Beatty.

CHAPTER

Seventeen

"*My name is Michael Anthony Hawkes. I have been searching for my birth family since 1995 through St. Patrick's Guild (SPG) in Dublin,*" I began.

I later added, "*....Through my search, I have recently obtained the death certificate of a woman, Elizabeth (Eilish) Mancell, whom I have recently learned was most likely my natural sister. You were listed on her record as the informant and a cousin....*"

I didn't want to sound like a scam artist. I wanted to gain Thomas Beatty's trust quickly. So, I included photos of from the orphanage and photos of me and Susan and our family, as well as copies of adoption paper trail documents and copies of the documents that led to Mr. Beatty. I wanted to make sure I came off as sincere. I wasn't sure how my intrusion into his life would be received. Would he and the rest of the relatives see me as the unwanted child that was sent to America? I was well aware of the culture that could deny me any entrance to their lives. But it was worth a try.

Two weeks later, to my absolute delight, I received an email in return, just before Christmas 2013, from Thomas

Anthony (Tony) Beatty, 83-year-old first cousin of my mother, Elizabeth!

Dear Michael,

I have received your letter regarding my late cousin Elizabeth (Betty) Mancell. I may be of some help to you as my mother and Betty's mother were sisters. I do recall my mother, some years after these events, telling me about Betty having twins. To my knowledge, all of this was kept from the Cleary family, including Betty's mother. I, being the youngest male in my family at the time, was also unaware of the event. However, my sister Maura, who is now 93, may have been closer to Betty and may also have some information which may be helpful to you. I will speak to her and advise her of your letter. In the meantime, please feel free to call me and I can fill you in on the Cleary side of the family.

Trusting I can be of help.
Tony Beatty.

Tony had a rare sense of not just duty to family connections, but a love for them. He was my birth mother's first cousin. I imagined his qualities were a family trait: accepting, trusting, kind, and accommodating. He had every right to brush me aside. Instead, he embraced me.

In a subsequent phone call, Tony shared, "If my mother were involved, I am convinced, so was Maura! She was the same age as Betty and as a young woman was close to your mother. I have never discussed this with her! She is a bit hard of hearing and thus doesn't talk on the phone, but I will be seeing her at Christmas and I will talk to her to see if she knows anything of your birth and early life."

I was so moved by his openness. He had been a Catholic all his life, and although he was angry at the Church's horrible abuse of power, he still believed in God, and the goodness of humanity. He was one of the best human beings I'd ever met.

When he asked Maura if she knew about Betty and her twins, Maura began to tear up. Maura related to Tony the details of her husband Eddie having spotted Betty and the tiny twins on the Ferry back to Dublin. Maura had had them in her home. Even though she was eight months pregnant at the time with her youngest child, she had even contemplated adopting the twins herself, but was understandably not in a position to do so. She shared that Betty had not intended that anyone from the family ever know of the twins. As luck or providence would have it, Eddie was on that boat—the very ferry trip that my mother was on to take the babies to Dublin. Betty had tearfully asked Eddie to tell no one. He convinced Betty to allow he and Maura and Maura's mother, Catherine to help her and the babies.

Maura had worried about what had become of the twins for the last 55 years. She and her daughter watched the Irish television programs regularly on adoption and finding and reuniting adoptees with long lost natural families. All the time I had been searching, Maura had been watching the adoption stories, hoping to hear about Betty's twins.

In early January—two weeks after our conversation— we received a package from Tony and Maura. I sat in my home office holding the package, my hands trembling. I called Susan as tears welled up in my eyes. I had, in most ways, come to grips with what I had been through. But I had not yet fully explored where I came from. I had longed for connection my entire life. Here was a package from Ireland that contained answers. But I couldn't open it alone. I was too overcome with emotion.

Susan dashed home from work to be with me. She was so excited for this piece of me to be restored. Together, we carefully opened this package that took so long to arrive. We pulled out a stack of black and white photographs. I held in my hands a photo of my mother. The resemblance was astounding. Her hair swept back and high in the style of the day, but her eyes were kind and she wore the expression on her face that so often looked back at me when I looked in the mirror and pondered who I was.

"My mother. I've found my mother."

The pent up emotional release was immediate. The feelings of being "less than" and the loneliness I had hidden for so long seemed to dissipate. I longed to sit with my mother and ask so many questions. She was lovely in the photo, taken when she was in her mid-twenties. It had been 55 years since I passed through the red door of relinquishment. It felt as though I was going back out that door into the sunlight.

We maintained our correspondence with Tony and continued plans for our trip to Ireland that would occur in March. Tony began taking genealogy lessons in his village and was investigating Betty's maternal and paternal genealogy. We shared with Tony how we found the Adoption Rights Alliance Search Angel and that she had uncovered the death certificates that led to finding him. Tony and the Search Angel were put in contact with one another.

Tony asked the SA for advice as to how to search for daughters of Betty's older brother Donal Cleary, also Tony's first cousin. Donal had died of tuberculosis in 1948, leaving a young widow, Mary, and three young daughters. The daughters, Tony indicated to the SA, had been placed in Goldenbridge Industrial School, never to be heard from again. A Google search revealed accusations that Goldenbridge had been an establishment rife with abuse and scandal.

The SA, in Dublin, continued to investigate online databases and Dublin support groups she knew of, for people who had been detained as children in Goldenbridge. Susan was searching online from California. The birth records of Donal's daughters, Marie, Dierdre, and Noreen, were found. No further records emerged. Did they survive Goldenbridge Orphanage?

Just like the Magdalene Laundries, many orphanages run by the Catholic Church were thought to be homes for the offspring of fallen women. They were given no kindness, only punishment for their mother's sins. Stark, medieval places of labor and penance, the Goldenbridge Industrial School was no different.

Children as young as six-years-old labored in dank, austere rooms creating rosaries. The work was tedious and if quotas were not met children were whipped. Marie-Therese O'Loughlin, a survivor of Goldenbridge in the 50s and 60s writes in her memoir: "Children often got temperamental and turned on each other. On the spot punishment by staff was an everyday event. Children had to stand on a cold landing (sometimes barefoot and wearing only slips) during the night for punishment. They were relentlessly flogged with thick bark from a tree by the nun in charge, if, for example, they had not fulfilled their quota of rosary beads in the factory. A quantity of older children worked on the quota for whole nights, wearing sleeveless nightdresses and no sandals. We constantly rocked backwards and forwards in our desks as we worked. This had a dual purpose: self-soothing and hurrying to get the work finished. It always achieved its aim. We could block out everything. We also resorted to this type of behaviour collectively with other children at the same time, as we always had the idea that we would get our work done faster. Rocking, banging heads, sucking thumbs and fingers, also occurred when we decided to give ourselves a break for a few minutes.

There was immeasurable pressure on the children to reach mandatory targets. Children were punished there and then on the spot; they were pinched on the arms, or they got a dig of the pliers if they didn't produce the prearranged amount on time; beads were flung back at them if there was deemed to be a fault.

The nervous tension haunted every day of our lives. We had not a solitary human being we could unburden our hearts to, we had to keep everything to ourselves; children would go into convulsions to rid themselves of pent-up anger." http://www.butterfliesandwheels.org/2006/the-goldenbridge-secret-rosary-bead-factory/

The Irony in all this is at the time, the Catholic Church was asking for donations for the needy children of Africa while the children of Goldenbridge Industrial School, under the watchful eyes of the Sisters of Mercy, were forced into labor, abused, and fed a ration of two slices of bread a day and one cup of brownish liquid called cocoa with no sugar in it.

Journalist and playwright Jason O'Toole interviewed the Archbishop of Armagh and Catholic Primate of All Ireland for Hot Press in 2016. In the interview, the Archbishop defends marriage as being between a man and a woman and also states: "I cannot understand how we as a country would want to remove that which is such a powerful expression of the equality of the right to life for all people—the most vulnerable. What it does call on us to do in Ireland is to be a place of compassion and care for everyone who is struggling."

A place of compassion and care for everyone who is struggling? Again, the Catholic Church deflects the immorality of it's past with present platitudes. The failure to admit past mistakes is mindboggling. The Church would be unapologetic for the treatment of girls at Goldenbridge. And under the extreme circumstances we uncovered there, I can't imagine three little girls surviving.

CHAPTER

Eighteen

*T*hrough the same Adoption Alliance Rights group, where we were blessed to find the Search Angel as an active participant, a request came looking for Irish adoptees who would share their story with the BBC. They were developing a documentary about the 2,100 Irish adoptees sent to the US, as well as birth mothers' stories.

Martin Sixsmith and BBC producers, in conjunction with the BBC program, Our World, were in California for the Oscars as the movie Philomena, the Hollywood version of Sixsmith's book, was up for a Best Picture at the Oscars. They also were producing the documentary *Ireland's Lost Babies* and interviewing US Irish adoptees for the program. Our email communication with them was facilitated by the Adoption Rights Group's leaders. Arrangements were made to film me at my home regarding my search for family and heritage. I told them that Susan and I were traveling to Ireland a few weeks later for the first time in 53 years, since I had been taken out of Ireland by Monsignor Hawkes. I also suggested that they Google Monsignor Benjamin Hawkes. I shared that my uncle, posthumously, had been accused by multiple adult men of abusing them as altar boys. I even told them of the conversation I had with Cardinal Mahony about the pending victims' lawsuit to give credence to the allegations.

I have never wanted to sound like I had some kind of vengeance, or that I was simply bitter and wanted the Catholic Church to look bad. I wanted the truth to be known. I believe in God, and I also knew that leadership in the Catholic Church had created a deep state of perversion, maltreatment, and cover-ups. I wanted to be factual, not emotional. Evil should never be swept under the carpet.

Monsignor Hawkes was now nearly thirty years dead. I wasn't ready to share my own history of having been molested with his immediate family and friends, let alone the wider world that would be reached through the documentary.

The LA Times article quotes one of the accusers as saying: "'Even though he is dead, I believe the Archdiocese should be aware of Msgr. Hawkes' actions….The man that I trusted and respected as a mentor and spiritual father took advantage of his position and left me with a traumatic experience to deal with."

In the late 1970s and early 1980s, he had been an altar boy at St. Basil's. His single mother couldn't afford to send him to Catholic school, but Hawkes said he would pay tuition at the junior seminary. In return, he had to work every Saturday and Sunday in the church. It was on those days, he said, that Hawkes molested him.

"He never let me forget he was paying for my tuition," he told church officials later. "Monsignor had a way of subduing someone so you'd feel like nothing."

The man brought his therapist to the meeting and informed officials that he wanted his experience documented so others would be believed if they came forward.

Five years later, a second man phoned the church's longtime lawyer. John McNicholas recognized the caller's name. He had been an altar boy at St. Basil's and, with Hawkes' help, had gone to college and law school. He now held a prominent position in law enforcement. "Msgr. Hawkes abused me," he told the lawyer.

McNicholas recently confessed, ""I was stunned,"

At a meeting with top archdiocese officials, the man, a veteran of years of undercover work, sobbed. The abuse, he said, started when he was twelve and lasted a full decade, rare considering Monsignor Hawkes preferred young boys. My guess is that the Monsignor needed to keep hold on this boy. He did, after all, try and get me into the shower when I was in college.

The young man said it began with the priest's hand in his pants when he was dressing for Mass, but escalated into Hawkes pinning him naked on a bed in the rectory and ejaculating on him. He eventually became strong enough to fight Hawkes off, but the Monsignor was still making unwanted advances until the week he died. Even I was shocked. The Monsignor became so brazen, so perverted, so desperate that not only did he keep up the abuse until the victim was in his early twenties, he tried repeatedly to satiate himself on this poor man until the day he died. I imagined The Monsignor's heart stopping in mid-grope. And I was again horrified that he had held my child.

The victim said that as a teen, he tried repeatedly to quit his job in the rectory. Each time the Monsignor would tell the victim's parents, struggling immigrants who spoke little English, that their son would lose his tuition and his chance to be successful in America. In a subsequent sworn statement to church lawyers, the victim recalled a

1975 incident when he locked himself in a bathroom to
avoid Hawkes:

> *"He grabbed me by the throat and told me how*
> *dare I had [locked] the doors. He put his hands on*
> *my genital area...and said, this is like mine because*
> *I am your father and I am taking care of you."*

The man's story of grooming and shame and abuse
was similar to mine. He took the boy to fancy restaurants
and vacations and made it clear that he "owned" him.

Emotionally, I just couldn't put that all on film, not
yet. I wanted to talk about my search, not my past. In the
end, the producer asked me off camera if I too had been
abused by Monsignor Hawkes. I told him that I had been
but was not ready to share this publicly.

The producers asked to film us once we were in Ireland
as part of the documentary. Their plan was to capture me on
tape visiting my mother's grave for the first time and walking
the streets of Dublin on St. Patrick's Day. I was excited to get
the experience on film, but nervous about how it would go. I
wanted to be protective of any relatives we met. I didn't want
them to think this whole effort was to exploit them.

Just before we were to leave for Ireland, we received a
response letter with attached documents from Sister Edith
of St. Patrick's Guild. The information was scant, but we did
receive some corroborating information. It was verified that
we had been relinquished to the Catholic Protection and
Rescue Society of Ireland at the age of five months and that
we were separated at that point, having been taken from our
birth mother, by a "court order," and placed in Irish Catholic
industrial schools in Kilkenny and then Dublin.

I had previously sent Sister Edith email questions regarding my birth father. Attempting to force the hand of Saint Patrick's Guild, I insinuated that my mother's estranged husband James might be the biological father after all, and if that were the case, the adoptions had been illegal. I emphasized "might be" hoping to put the fear of God into them.

I further told them we had found people in Dublin—maternal family who had known Betty and had provided more of the story from them. Sister Edith replied;

> *"In your email message of December 5, you mention an acquaintance of Eilish, your late sister, and you also speak of a cousin 'on the Cleary side'—It might be helpful if I could speak to these people? I'm not sure, but perhaps it would enable us to draw some threads together if they would allow you to pass on addresses or phone numbers?*
>
> *On December 31 you referred to 'another person in Dublin' who had known your birthmother and had perhaps known your birth father also. Would it be possible to have a name, address and/or telephone number for that person? It would be helpful to have a word with him/her"*

I knew immediately what the motive was. I believe she wanted to intimidate practicing Catholic family members into remaining silent. They knew there were legal incongruities in the adoption of thousands of babies and they were in full damage control mode. I wasn't about to facilitate their cover up and I definitely wanted to protect

the good people who had been so helpful to me. Blood is
thicker than holy water. I told her "no." I wish I had told
her Hell No!

The tact of seeking out a connection to Betty's first
husband put a little more pressure on Sister Edith. The
letter included a statement that "the father" had responded
in a letter directly to the sister-in Charge of St. Patrick's
Home, Kilkenny through his solicitor in England. Sister
Edith stated: *"In the letter the father confirmed that he was
the father of the twins and that he raised no objection to them
being adopted."* Sister Edith continued, *"He had been advised
by his solicitor that he was under no obligation to make such a
statement and that no pressure was being put on him to do so."*

The attachments to the Saint Patrick's Guild letter
included the marriage certificate of Betty and her husband
James, the Certificate of Surrender and Consent of Mother,
signed by Betty, and a copy of Betty's affidavit, indicating
that her husband was not the father of the twins.

Also included was a copy of the page from the register
at St. Patrick's Boys School, Kilkenny. It listed the "charge"
of, "not having any home" and the "sentence of detention" as
until "April 27, 1974", the day before we would turn 16 years
old. The document missing was the letter from the solicitor of
"the father" presumably, because it would have listed a name.

The tact worked. St. Patrick's Guild representatives
found themselves in the awkward position of having to
prove the adoption was legal without giving away who
the real father was. I didn't get what I wanted most—my
biological father's name. But he had signed a document
that was provided by his solicitor, and that was gold. It
meant somewhere in their files my father's name existed.
I just had to pry it out of them.

CHAPTER

Nineteen

I was nervous, but equally uncertain and confused. We had been saving for this trip for a while. It had seemed a fantasy at first, a fictional quest that would probably end in disappointment. When it became real, I wasn't sure how to feel.

I had to rely on humor to cope, so I joked with Susan: "What do you think we'll find behind door number three?"

When we finally sat down in our seats, I was emotionally exhausted after fifty-three years of wondering and, 19 years of searching. I was grateful to be sitting next to Susan. She was Professor Robert Langdon in Angels and Demons—indefatigable, full of faith and encouragement.

As we sat on the plane and thought of the many nights Susan sat at the computer until early morning searching obscure records, sending letters, talking to genealogical groups, and corresponding with the Search Angel, and then, blood relatives. Love is a powerful motivator and it's quite humbling when somebody takes up your cross.

Another irony in this journey is that it took several years to get a passport, because it took so long to prove that I had been legally adopted in America and was a naturalized citizen. in 1986 President Reagan signed amnesty legislation that legalized nearly 3 million undocumented immigrants, a subsequent act was passed specifically for the undocumented Irish babies illegally adopted to the US and living in all fifty states. Still, it was difficult to sort through the paperwork and prove that I was a US citizen.

It was nighttime in London when we landed and found our connecting flight to Dublin. In the dark of night, we flew out of Heathrow, over the black vast sea of Ireland, two people among billions looking for a single life in all those humans. My thoughts turned to my mother and the stories we got from her cousins Tony and Maura.

We were only taking a short flight from London to Dublin. But my mother, we had learned from Tony and Maura, had taken a four-hour night ferry, then more hours on a train to London. The first trip from Dublin to hide the pregnancy; a journey toward the unknown and the difficult delivery she endured was bad enough. The journey back with two four-month-old twins she loved deeply, knowing that she would soon have to say goodbye must have been unbearable. The emotional odyssey seemed nearly impossible to survive. The fear and the heartache became all too real as I contemplated the loss of my own little son.

When the plane touched down in Dublin, and I stepped off, I thought, "Fifty-three years gone and now I am finally home for the first time since I was a toddler." The feeling was surreal and overwhelmingly poignant. Did my mother know that I had made it home? I hoped that she could feel it.

We took a taxi to our hotel, the Westbury, off Grafton Street. I was the illegitimate son, yet my cousin Tony had been nothing but kind and welcoming. I phoned to tell him we arrived safely.

The next morning, bright and early, we headed to the hotel restaurant for the fabled Irish Breakfast. It was delicious; however I can't say that blood sausage is my thing! We then proceeded to the lobby anxious to meet the cousin who had graciously answered our letter only three months prior. It was extremely fortunate Tony's mother had informed him of the existence of Betty's twins. How blessed we felt that Tony and Maura had been so open to contact and had shared precious information and photos. We had no idea what Tony looked like. We hadn't thought to ask for a photo or description.

Across the lobby, we spotted an older, very well dressed, gentleman with white hair, approaching with a quick smile. I looked at him and he looked at me; without saying a word we embraced, and that spiritual family bond overwhelmed me. I don't remember many words from that moment. We had come to the Isle of Hope and Tony was our guide to my mother's half of the family tree. That was all that mattered.

Tony told us that his car was double-parked in front of the hotel, and he had asked the bellhop if he could leave the car there a moment as there was something incredibly special and important that he wanted to show us before we left for the day.

An exceedingly spry octogenarian, Tony led us briskly down Anne Street, a very short distance away from the hotel, where he paused before a building with an ornate red door. He told us that Maura had shared that this was the very door through which Catherine his mother had helped my mother Betty "relinquish" her twins to the Catholic Protection and Rescue Society of Ireland .

How incredible it was that we had made accommodations at that hotel, which was so close to the red door where my mother and Tony's mother last held us as babies. How fitting that we began our day where my story began, and where my mother had such a painful parting. As we walked back, I noted a statue of Phil Lynott from the rock band Thin Lizzy. His mother had kept him yet had to give up two other children to adoption. The horrors of single motherhood in Ireland in the 50s and 60s was gradually coming to light. Jason O'Toole interviewed Phil's mother on the anniversary of her son's death. She opened up for the first time, speaking about being banished to the slums and the mistreatment and the manipulative tactics of the nuns. Shortly after giving birth to Phillip, she was sent to the Selly Oak Home for unmarried mothers. She was 17 years old. "It was awful what they did to me in that place. They put me to work in the shed because I was the lowest of the low. It was freezing work." The nuns told her she could leave this chamber of horrors if she would give up her baby for adoption. All this was after a failed attempt at an abortion and running away from her family because she was shamed and ostracized. She eventually escaped and raised her child alone.

We had inadvertently landed in the midst of the big picture of Ireland's unwed mothers and lost babies. I again marveled at my mother's courage.

We hopped in the car with Tony as our guide, and off we went. The next stop was Synge Street, the home that Lizzie, my grandmother, owned, the home from which Betty had to flee in January of 1958, to hide her pregnancy. I marveled that Lizzie, a young widow, age 31, with five small children had eventually purchased the home and created a living for herself and her children in 1940's Ireland. Tony, along with his genealogy lessons, had researched all the residences at which our family had resided for three generations in Dublin.

We drove through the Upper Dorset neighborhood, where the cooperage and Cleary family flat had been in 1916. We visited St. Kevin's, the church in which Betty had been baptized, the church in which she had been married. It's a small stone church; the kind tourists take photos of. But inside is where Betty hid her shame until the last moment, when she had to flee. No one in the congregation, including her own mother, would have sat in those pews to comfort her. They simply didn't know.

We were taken to Mount Jerome Cemetery. After Lizzie's death in 1976, Betty, her sister Joan, and Eilish estranged themselves from extended family. Tony and Maura had not been made aware that Betty had died until well after her funeral. I thought of the potential loneliness of these three women, whom I might have met, had St. Patrick's Guild not put off my search attempts almost twenty years earlier. At the time of Eilish's car accident, Tony had been called, as her only known family. He had visited Eilish in the hospital before she died.

I wondered at the estrangement of Maura and Betty. It may have been too painful for Betty to be around Maura and her family. I also suspect that Betty suffered from depression. How could she not having experienced such profound loss? The world had closed in on her the day she stepped off the ferry back on Irish soil. Emotional isolation may have been her survival tactic.

The enormous Mount Jerome Cemetery, in Harold's
Cross, with over 200,000 burials, stretched before us like a sea
of dead. It was humbling. Tony, having planned and scoped
out the route of this tour, took us directly to Betty's grave.
After all these years, and hours of staring at the photograph
of my mother, I was standing at her grave. I knew of her
struggles, her mother's struggles to take care of her. I knew of
her daughter, Eilish and her lonely life and untimely death.
I knew of my biological father and his relationship with my
mother that started the whole journey. And I was standing
with my cousin at Bettys' grave. So many lives intertwined,
and so much love and acceptance from Irish relatives by
blood whom I was just getting to know and love. Such a stark
contrast from my adoptive family who you would expect to
love us but only treated us as second-class human beings. And
here was family through a socially unacceptable relationship,
embracing us.

The afternoon was damp. The grounds sodden. The
grayness of the stone matched the sky. Yet I was closer to
my mother than I had ever been, and it felt as though a
light was finding its way into my soul.

Betty's grave was a four-person deep family plot. First
was Lizzie, the grandmother we as babies were hidden
from, then my mother Betty, then Joan, Betty's younger
sister, then Eilish only two years earlier. We left flowers
and had a silent prayer at the grave. Later, in a scene of
great redemption, Tony would sign ownership of the
grave over to me, the illegitimate grandson, who had been
hidden and banished from family and country. It was a
beautiful gesture, which left me teary-eyed. I felt like I had
returned to a grand circle of family. He then informed me
that he had commissioned a proper headstone.

Tony then drove us to Black Rock, Temple Hill; we were in search of St. Patrick's, the holding pen that my sister and I had been brought to in preparation for adoption.

We travelled the narrow country roads and tight streets of towns feeling like we were moving through a maze looking for side roads that would lead us into an openness of understanding.

As we bumped along in Tony's small car, we came across a stately building that turned out to be a retirement home for nuns. A sign in the drive stated, "Do Not Enter."

"You didn't come this far to let a sign stop you," Tony said, without so much as touching the brakes.

I loved his bravado. This undeterred Irishman with thick white hair and flannel trousers that fortified him against the damp. He had taken up our quest.

So off Tony drove through the gates and down the road to the old estate and eased to a stop in front of medieval looking wooden doors.

I unfolded myself from the small car and strode confidently toward the building. I knocked loudly.

After a little while, a tiny, incredibly old nun came to the door.

"Had this building ever been St. Patrick's Temple Hill? I asked.

"No," came the response from a face with a thousand wrinkles. But she kindly invited us into the parlor and gave us a little history of the place.

"Could you help me with the location of these photos?" I asked, showing her the photos sent to Bill and Helen before they agreed to adopt us.

She examined the photo of me as a three-year-old next to a nun whose face was cloaked in shadow. My face looked defiant and a bit scared. But in the background was St. Patrick's Temple Hill. The old nun squinted at the background and recognized the facility.

"Yes, I know where this is," she said and gave us directions to the facility.

We drove a bit, amazed at our good luck, and joked that we had just met the oldest living nun in Ireland.

"This is it," Tony said, pulling up to a fence.

The location was in the process of being converted into luxury condominiums. Once again, the stories of obscene abuse would be hidden behind opulence. I remembered something Monsignor Hawkes said: "The rich have souls too."

The fence was too high to climb but I found a hole to peer through. I could see the building beyond the construction site. It was dark gray and foreboding. I recognized the front entrance from the 1961 photos. But memories of this time in my life would not come. Most of my first three years were dark, an empty drawer.

I stared at the stone building and the grounds for a long time, trying to see myself on the steps, on the lawn, inside one of the rooms. Nothing. All I could conjure up was my fear of safety pins. I had read of accounts of people working in places like St. Patrick's. Their practice was to pin babies down to their cot mattresses with safety pins through their bedclothes. In this way, babies were held fast, unable to move about their cribs, and never swaddled and loved. I look at the photo of me and my sister standing with the nun in front of this building. I notice the tight grip the nun has on my wrist so that I was unable to move.

The next part of the tour with Tony was Howth, where our common ancestor, Tony's grandmother, my great grandmother, Mary Gill nee Reilly, nee Kavanagh, and Tony's grandfather had all lived. We couldn't pass through without sampling the fish and chips, of course. Battered and fried to perfection.

John Gill had been a very skilled mason; whose specialty was steeple making. He spent years on the steeple of a church in Howth. It struck me how many generations gave so much of their lives to the Church. Lizzie and Catherine and two younger brothers had spent most of their childhoods at that residence.

Tony and I had a moment to talk about abuse among the priests. Tony was still a practicing Catholic, but he confessed: "It makes me angry, to tell the truth. Priests behaving that way."

We talked about the role of priests and their vows to teach of Christ.

"Do you think times are different now than they were then?" I asked him.

"I hope so," he answered wishfully. "I hope so."

Somehow, people like Betty and Lizzie and Tony and Eddie and Maura, they survive. Spiritually they see the unfairness and hypocrisy in a religious institution and somehow manage to keep the institution separate from their devotion to God. The world and all its institutions are unfair, even licentious. So one must learn to have faith in a being not a system, society, or organization.

After our emotional family history tour, Tony had plans for the evening. We went back into the city centre to that second place of Irish worship—the pub. The Six Nations rugby match between Ireland and France was on and you never watch a match alone. If Ireland were to win, they would solidify England's loss of the tournament. The

Irish still revel in any loss suffered by the English. It was a big deal. Near the end of the raucous match, on the big screen in a classic Irish pub, minutes to go, and things were tense. Tony, seeking any form of divine intervention he could find, turned to Susan, obviously the most likely in the pub to be able to summon divine intervention, and yelled over the crowd, "Pray to whomever you pray to Susan!"

Susan must have done something right because Ireland won the match and the tournament—they were the champions of Europe. What a momentous day it had been, one I believe had been guided by a provident hand, right down to the final matches of a rugby game.

The next morning, Sunday, Tony picked us up early and we headed back to the church that Betty and Eilish would have attended. Here the plan had been to meet Maura for the first time. The loyalty of Maura to my mother was remarkable. Irish society would have destroyed Betty. Maura was a saint for taking care of her and guarding her secret, even during the years of separation.

We met Maura and her daughter Moira in the church's parking lot. Immediately upon looking at Maura, I could see the kindness in her eyes. She was a beautiful and elegant woman, appearing younger than her 93 years, somewhat frail, hair of white, and walking with a cane. She was in a skirt, sweater, and pearls; respectfully dressed for Mass.

Moira, her lovely daughter, was six months younger than me and my sister. Moira had been the baby that Maura carried, and had been close to delivering, when Maura had taken Betty on walks with the babies and watched them lie together on the floor of their Dublin home. Many years had gone by before Maura told Moira about us. I think she may have worried that the secret would die with her. She wanted a reunion of some kind. Together Maura and Moira had watched adoption and long-lost family stories on the television, knowing that Betty's twins were out there somewhere.

I extended my arm to Maura, and was delighted when she took hold of my elbow, and with Moira on the other side; we helped her up the steps into the church. We settled into a pew just in time for Mass. There was a lovely family choir that sang hymns of praise to God. It was an emotional moment, envisioning Betty in this church, as an elderly woman. I imagined her sitting beside me, beside Maura in that spot where she may have habitually sat for years. Finally, the shame would be lifted from her. I prayed that Betty could see us together in this church, a connection that began so long ago, a redemption for Betty and closure for Maura.

After mass, we walked Maura out of the church, helping her into the car, driven by Moira, with the plan to meet at the Westbury hotel. I had made reservations with the hotel for a small private tearoom where we ordered sandwiches, tea, and coffee. This was the first time we had an opportunity to really sit down and visit. The tearoom, with its fine furnishings was a far cry from the home my mother grew up in—simple and sparsely decorated.

Maura began to tell stories about my mother and the family. Betty and Maura were not only first cousins; they were exactly the same age and the best of friends as children and young women. According to Maura, my mother was an outgoing individual and Maura was the quiet one. As Maura spoke, she constantly looked me in the eyes with a kindness that ran deep.

Maura shared that we little twins were hidden in Maura's house from Betty's mother and that Maura, and her mother Catherine had, during the daytime, been able to take Betty and the babies out of the Regina Coeli Hostel, an austere homeless shelter for women and their children. At one point in the conversation, Maura said, "You know, Betty had no choices. She would have loved to have met you."

Tears welled up in Susan's and my eyes at the kindness of this sweet woman. She had a faith and strength that was hard to describe, and to reward her with a visit was a privilege beyond words. We listened intently to the details of Betty's heart wrenching story. Maura also revealed that she was certain that Betty's estranged husband James was not the biological father; that our father had been, "a Dublin guy." Tony said that he had seen Betty with the man he suspected was my father, walking on a street one late 1950's evening in Dublin.

My mother's sorrow became mine. I felt overwhelmed. I felt healed. I felt connected. I had discovered cousins who loved my mother and the sweet woman who helped and loved us as babies and kept Betty's secret beyond the day she died. I soaked in the details of their lives, of my mother's life, of an entire family tree that had somehow found me.

The next day was St. Patrick's Day. 500,000 people lined the streets of Dublin for the parade. The BBC producers turned their cameras on the chaos, Tony and I walking together like tourists. It was a cheesy shot, but the producer liked it. Marching bands passed us from California and Louisiana. Tony and his family stated that Dubliners rarely attend the St. Patrick's Day parade as it was mostly a tourist activity. I thought it was a bit ironic that Irish tradition had been taken over by European students mostly looking for a reason to party. But Tony didn't seem to mind. It was all good "craic" to him. Almost on cue, the drizzle thickened. I turned to Susan and we were both smiling uncontrollably. "The Irish make everything better, don't they?"

The following day, we met at the Westbury with the dear Adoption Rights Alliance Search Angel, the Irish adoptee and genealogist who found Eilish's death certificates and made finding my family possible. The SA was one of those people who selflessly delights in the research, of finding bits and clues that connect people to their families.

We had arranged, the following day, a meeting with Sister Edith of St. Patrick's Guild, which was a miracle in itself. She'd given us the run around in every communication and must have been torn between giving adoptees like me what they needed to connect with their biological families, and protecting the Catholic Church. I briefly empathized with her position, but reviewing the communications on the way over I decided she was a sycophant left at the crime scene holding the bag.

We drove over with the BBC producers. St. Patrick's Guild was a notorious organization to many in the Adoption Rights Alliance Group and to many whom had researched the treatment of unwed mothers, trafficking of babies, or banished babies of Ireland. The BBC wanted to film me entering the building. I didn't want to risk refusal and a slammed door. We compromised with a shot taken from across the street, the camera hidden in the bushes.

So off we went through a string of pastoral towns outside of Dublin toward St. Patrick's Guild, which I affectionately called the Little Shop of Horrors.

I was surprised at the size of the property of St. Patrick's Guild. Expansive lawns unrolled away from a large complex of older buildings. A chapel rested between the old building and more modern structures forming a campus. My first thought was that donors were still supporting this place, unawares of what went on.

We parked the car and while walking to the door of St. Patrick's Guild offices, I thought about my own young grandchildren who had been raised by loving parents. I thought of those trusting little faces that arrived here, starving for affection. I knew they would never be held in loving arms, receiving reassurance as they navigated toddlerhood. My first three years were of neglect. No wonder I drew a complete blank in memories, only feelings of despair. As each of my grandchildren hit the milestones of five months, then three-and-a-half years, I had noted with some inner sadness how these young babies had been so attached to their parents; something I had missed. Something every child that passed through this medieval place was deprived of.

When a child is passed from person to person in an industrial school, or holding pen, without the opportunity to bond with people who will always be there, how do you learn to trust the world?

CHAPTER

Twenty

St. Patrick's Guild was a cold and emotionless place, with stone buildings that felt eternally unforgiving. But in there was a secret, the name of my birth father. And I was determined to get it, to retrieve one scrap of humanity from the place.

I knocked on the Gothic door. It seemed to echo in my brain. Within a few moments, We were met by a young woman. She welcomed us graciously and ushered us to a small room with monastic furnishings—a small table and chairs. I had a flash of foreboding, the kind of feeling I had while waiting in a similar room at Sacred Heart Elementary where the head nun would soon strong arm me over the table and beat my behind with a paddle.

The door opened and in walked a smaller, serious looking older woman with short-cropped gray hair, wearing an austere skirt and sweater. She introduced herself as Sister Edith. Sister Edith was the representative of the organization that had stalled the search not once, but several times, and had given false and misleading information. We brought with us a brief case with all records of previous correspondence and a photo album with copies of the 1961 photos of that had my sister and I that had been sent to the Hawkes' family as well as photos of Betty.

Sister Edith sat down at a small table opposite from us. It was a tense moment. The inquisition. Sister Edith held firmly to a brown folder. She set it carefully on the table in front of her, out of our reach. We entered into a pleasant, disarming conversation, asking many questions, some of which we knew the answer to and some things we wanted confirmed. Yes, I had been a resident of St. Patrick's. Yes, I had been adopted. Yes, I wanted to know my mother...and my father.

Sister Edith was evasive, trying to sense what we already knew without giving up much information herself. After 20 minutes of this, Susan had a tickle in her throat and started coughing.

Sister Edith asked, "Can I get you some water?"

"Yes please, that would be really nice," Susan replied.

As the nun left, she closed the door behind her. To my amazement, she left the folder on the table. Susan, still coughing, immediately stood and opened the folder.

"There has to be something here that she isn't telling us!" she said.

I was only a little shocked, but not surprised. Actually, I found it quite entertaining at the same time. I bent my head below the table and watched the light under the door as if I could see footsteps coming while Susan rummaged through official Catholic paperwork without authorization.

It's a trivial thing, I know now. The worst thing they could do was shut up all the files and ask us to leave. It's probably what they were going to do anyway. But the

PTSD from my early school days made me sweat and shake like the next person in line for the hangman.

To Susan's chagrin, the folder only contained copies of the recent email correspondence and the letter that Sister Edith had sent to us a few weeks ago. Susan sat down, still coughing, as Sister Edith entered with a little pitcher of water and glass on a tray. The sleuth graciously thanked Sister Edith for the water.

Sister Edith also had an additional folder with her.

From the second folder she produced copies of a decades old Catholic publication outlining the history of St. Patrick's Blackrock, Temple Hill where my sister and I spent three months prior to the adoptions. According to the copies of the article, the facility had been for a time a pediatric nurse training site. It was an attempt to put a little positive PR on the place, and at the same time defer any wrongdoing since the students were rotated through regularly and who could possibly know if children had been treated improperly? Something that was easy to apologize for while staying morally detached.

My thoughts were, *How could Sister Edith think this a positive aspect of the facility?* It was another example of upheaval that young children would experience, as their caregivers rotated through every few weeks with no chance to bond. But I smiled at the stories, and Susan and I played polite.

When Sister Edith finished, I produced a photo of my mother stating, "Without your assistance, we have found first cousins of our mother, including those who helped her hide us as she was preparing to relinquish my sister and me." Original correspondence from St. Patrick's Guild stated that only my mother's mother had been aware of the pregnancy and births." Susan produced the letter. "This is not true according to the family. Betty's mother had no idea her daughter was pregnant and planning on giving up her babies."

Sister Edith leaned back. "A detail Betty would have shared with us. I don't know the reason she would state that."

"And," Susan continued. "The father also knew she was giving up the babies."

Well," sister Edith said. "We have no record of the father."

"Do you know why there was a court order for Betty to relinquish the babies?"

"Betty signed the papers, as all mothers do. She would have known it was the only way for them to escape the bondage of a fallen mother."

I steamed at this. Living with my fallen mother would have been better than a childhood of beatings and abuse. "Are you aware that my future adopted uncle, Right Reverend Benjamin Hawkes apparently found me in Ireland during his visit during the 1961 Patrician year celebrations?"

With this, Sister Edith perked up and said, "I met your uncle once!"

"Yes," I said. "A very powerful man. Is that why the adoption was expedited?"

"A man of his stature could get things done," Sister Edith said proudly, as if a man of God needed no rules.

"Yes, he could," Susan said. "No vetting necessary."

"Because of whom your uncle was, he would have been able to cut through the red tape."

And there it was. The first case against the Catholic Church. No government documents necessary. No vetting of adopting families. Bill and Helen were 46 when my sister and I were placed into their home. Far too old to meet the requirements of a legal adoption.

I pressed forward. "Do you have any idea how sad I find it, that my mother was denied the ability to know, in the last years of her life, that her children were OK?"

Sister Edith belligerently answered, "Her faith would have carried her through."

I wasn't going to let her off that easily. "I find it incredibly despicable that while we waited in the queue for St. Patrick's Guild to get back to us, my mother died not knowing that we were OK."

Edith had no response.

Susan drew out a copy of my birth certificate. "On Michael's birth certificate, Elizabeth's married name is listed. She was not divorced at the time. I wonder if her husband knew his children were being adopted. As a married woman, adoption of the babies would have been illegal."

"An affidavit was sent that stated otherwise," sister Edith stated matter-of-factly.

"So Mr. Mancell gave up his babies, or they were adopted out illegally?"

Sister Edith paused.

"Our recent correspondence stated that you have a document that lists the name of my father," I said, going in for the kill.

Sister Edith knew she could no longer hide facts from us. She had to prove that we were not the product of Betty and her legal estranged husband. Sister Edith slowly opened the folder and, at last, produced a document and sat it on the table. I picked it up and read out loud:

Dear Madam,

*We have been consulted by Mr. Patrick Ryan of 3
Willow Court, Leagrave, Luton, who has shown us
your letter of October 2nd, 1960, addressed to Mrs.
Mancell. Mr. Ryan has told us that he raises no
objection to his two children, and whose mother is
Mrs. Mancell, being adopted and he acknowledges
that he is the father of these children.*

Yours faithfully,
Currall and Randall

After 19 years of searching, we finally had a name:
Patrick Ryan. The letter from his solicitor remarkable gave
us a 1960 address of my father.

"That's all I have," Sister Edith said.

Every third boy in Ireland is named Patrick. And
Ryan is also a common surname. Sister Edith smirked.

"We named our fifth child Ryan!" Susan said.

The smirk on Sister Edith's face deepened.

CHAPTER

Twenty-One

That evening, at the hotel, Susan began searching the 1911 Ireland census records. We had a name, my father's name. Was it a complete birth name? We had a Luton, England address. Tony and Maura were certain that he was a "Dublin guy," but was he born in Dublin? Did he even live in Dublin in 1911, as a three-year-old? There were over 100 Patrick Ryan's in the Dublin area as listed in the 1911 Irish census, who were between the ages of two and four. The hunt would have to wait until we got home.

The next day, the self-guided green blur tour, as organized by the travel agent we had worked with, began in earnest. We took a taxi to the rental car lot and picked up our reserved car. I was driving. Susan was navigating. I practiced driving on the left side for a bit in the parking lot, turning incorrectly several times.

I pulled out of the exit of the rental lot and immediately turned into oncoming traffic! The roundabouts were killer! The mantra became, "To the left, to the left!" We spent ten adventurous days driving from Dublin to Waterford, then onto Killarney, and to Clifden. My inner navigation was off. For years I had known one way to be, one way to drive. I had to retrain my self. It was invigorating, full of laughs and mishaps, and close calls. But it was also metaphorical, learning how to be somebody else, somebody complete. I wanted to see the country the way my parents would have seen it, lived it.

We went back to Tony's research on the Cleary family for the days we had left in Ireland. He had discovered the address of the family home and cooperage on Upper Dorset in Dublin, as listed in the Irish Census of 1901 and 1911. Daniel and Honoria Cleary listed that they had had 13 children born alive, only seven were alive in 1911. Susan was able, once she had Wi-Fi in the hotels, to research the family further. She found the Clearys were from the area of South County Limerick. I wanted to stay in a castle we were booked for, to get a feel for the ancient history. Sadly, it wasn't possible. We took a two-day detour to South County Limerick.

We were able to find the church where Daniel Cleary and Honoria Casey Cleary, my great grandparents, had been married in 1885. This was the beginning of a rich history we would find of the Cleary and Casey lines. But this hunt would have to wait too. BBC producers wanted shots not dreary details of dusty relatives. Not to mention that I was relying on the GPS to find the Rock of Cashel but ended up in a farmer's barn yard.

Family history research in a foreign country, with records either guarded or lost, is an adventure. I wanted to know more than the ancestors that led up to my existence. I wanted to know their lives. I wanted to know the historical context that shaped their personalities, their resilience; and I wanted to know more about the blood bond that connected them so tightly. Tony was a cousin. I was the illegitimate son from America. Yet we both felt this familial bond and craving to know more.

The BBC producers asked if they could film us in Belfast, after hearing that Susan and I were booked to spend two days there. Plans were made to film during a "Black Cab Tour." The tour consisted of being met at the hotel by a former IRA member, an ex-political prisoner, to be toured around and schooled in the history of the Troubles. I mentioned to him that my grandmother, Lizzie Cleary, her mother-in-law, Honoria, and sister-in law Marie had been members of Cumann na mBan, a Republican women's paramilitary organization. It was gratifying to learn that I was a descendant of revolutionaries. Perhaps that's where I got my defiant streak that earned me stripes from the nuns and my adoptive father.

There was a mural in progress which was being created for the 100th anniversary commemoration of the organization of Cumann na mBan. At the mural, I was asked by the two artists if I would like to write my grandmother's name on it. I proudly wrote "Lizzie Cleary" on the mural.

"Do you know a good tattoo place?" I asked the artist.

Susan rolled her eyes. This new identity was growing on me. I had a clan. I had connection. I had protection. I was a proud descendent of a rebel.

My sister and I were successfully hidden from my grandmother Lizzie. I was proud to have it out in the open. I wish she could have been there to see it. I think Lizzie would have liked that, the rebel, and her grandchild.

After Belfast, we spent the last two days back in Dublin. Tony drove us to Mount Jerome, where we would see the Gravestone that Tony had commissioned. It was a beautiful memorial tribute to not only Betty, but to Eilish, Joan and Lizzie. The last day in Dublin, we met Maura and Moira at a restaurant in the town of Swords, north of Dublin city center. It was a pleasant gathering of family. Maura shared more insights and memories that she had of Betty.

During lunch, Maura would put her hand on mine. Here was the woman who helped care for me, wept when I was taken away, and prayed for me. I felt like I had known her my entire life, and that God knew her soul. It was a spiritually transcendent moment that only happens after years of wandering in the wilderness.

As we got up from dinner, I held Maura by the elbow. We got to the car and hugged. It was one of those sweet embraces that helps the healing process. Afterward, Maura turned and held Susan by the cheeks and pulled her close, looking into her eyes. "Betty would have loved you," she said.

We watched them walk away, knowing we might never see each other again. It's hard to express how grateful we were to meet some of those who had shared Betty's journey: Eddie and Maura, their mother Catherine, Tony. The clan. The bloodline.

I was heartsick at having to say goodbye; and wondered if we would ever be able to return. The next day, we flew from Dublin to JFK and on to Los Angeles. There were mixed emotions, smiles and a few tears reminiscing the last few weeks. I tried to put into words and sketches what we had experienced, but there was just too much to soak in. I would have to process the emotions first, and then organize the experiences into a story that made sense. I decided the story needed to start with Betty's journey, then my childhood, then the love of Susan and her drive to uncover the story. She became the angel on a mission! We make a good team. But I still wish I had gotten that tattoo.

We returned home to a new world. California, with all its modern buildings and mild climate; the Hollywood vibe is so different than the realness of Ireland. There's a history in Ireland that goes back thousands of years. Its thick on the walls of the pubs and you hear it in the accents of the people, each dialect an anchor to clans thousands of years old. California is a new settlement with little history. Over every conversation hangs a vision of the future. Ireland respects her history, honors those who forged the way. They have their heroes and their loyalties. I was seeking redemption, which sadly I could not achieve. But I had found reclamation, that gathering in that I had so desperately needed. It was enough for the time being.

Once home, Susan was off to the hunt. She pored over the documents that we had received from Sister Edith. One in particular was the registration log from St. Patrick's Kilkenny, which listed that I had been previously housed with my mother and sister at Regina Coeli Hostel. Susan wrote to Regina Coeli administrators and received a swift reply. The letterhead read, "Legion of Mary, Regina Coeli Hostel." The administrator shared information from their records. He confirmed that a woman named Betty Mancell was admitted to the hostel on 16 August 1958. The letter stated, "She gave her age as 37 and her address as 29 Synge Street, Dublin. She gave her religion as Catholic. She had come from London on the same date with her twins. They were born at Parkwell Hospital, Middlesex and baptized at St. Mary of Angels, Bayswater. She indicated she was separated from her husband for 10 years and had a girl of 9 years who was living with the girl's grandmother. 'The Crusade of Rescue' insisted on Betty coming home, wanted her to come before the birth of the children. She was hoping to get the twins adopted. Betty left the Regina Coeli Hostel on 18th September 1958."

"The Crusade of Rescue!" Another clue! Susan researched and found the Catholic Children's Society (Westminster) Crusade of Rescue. The society had a website application for adoption files; I applied for my file. Within a few weeks, a packet of documents arrived in the mail. The cover letter was a summary of records held by the Catholic Children's Society Crusade of Rescue. It read:

> *Your birth mother Elizabeth Mancell nee*
> *Cleary had an 8-year-old daughter, Eilish, of*
> *her marriage to Mr. Mancell. They married in*
> *Dublin 1948. Elizabeth was separated from*
> *her husband. Elizabeth told us that she met your*
> *father, Patrick Ryan, 3 years earlier in a ballroom*
> *in Dublin where she was working as a waitress.*
> *He played in the band there. Mr. Ryan is recorded*
> *as having worked on the railways. Elizabeth*
> *told us that he was married with 2 sons living in*
> *Ireland. Elizabeth told us that she intended to end*
> *the relationship with your father. At some point*
> *Elizabeth and Patrick came to London. I imagine*
> *that this may have been to keep her pregnancy*
> *secret. Elizabeth wrote to us for help in February*
> *1958. We contacted the Catholic Protection and*
> *Rescue Society of Ireland (CPRSI) in Dublin to see*
> *if they would be able to offer support / assistance*
> *with Elizabeth's request for your adoption.*

CPRSI administrators arranged for her and your admission to Regina Coeli in Dublin. You had lived with Elizabeth and Patrick at 15 Leinster Square, Bayswater, London until she took you to Dublin on 16th August 1958. We have no further information about Patrick.

Finally, we'd found somebody in the Catholic Church that had a heart. No politics, no cover up. The Catholic Children's Society Crusade of Rescue had nothing to hide. Their mission was to help children—now adults—and they were open about their records. What I have since come to understand is that there are some Catholic organizations with extraordinarily little oversight from the leadership of the church. They go about their missions unnoticed, some doing incredible work, and some abusing their power. The strict oversight of priests and monsignors carried unspoken rules to protect the name of the church at all costs. Unchecked power begets moral corruption. I was grateful that an organization in the church was operating without threat of intimidation, or if they were, courageous enough to pay no attention to it.

In addition to the cover letter and summary, letters confirming arrangements and responses to Betty's enquiries, three original, 1958, handwritten letters were included. In the letters, Betty wrote the following:

From Letter One:

I was living with my mother at home, and I left home leaving a letter saying I was going to work. If she knew the truth, it would kill her, and she would never let me home again, and I do want to see my little girl again.

Letter Two

*My babies are born, a girl and a boy, and both
perfect, a really good weight too. Please don't let
the hospital know. They are making a great fuss
of me, and the babies and I know they would be
very disappointed with me if they knew what I
intended doing. Could you write to me without
letting the hospital know? I will be here I'm sure
for about 8 or 10 days. I will not be able to go
to Cork, as I will not be well enough. I feel very
weak, neither can I afford to keep the babies. I
have no hope at all of keeping them with no money.
Could you take the babies until I am well enough
to work? I certainly can't go home to my mother. I
hope to hear from you soon. Please make it urgent.
Respectfully, Betty Mancell.*

Letter Three:

*Dear Secretary, could you please do something soon
about the adoption of my twins. Both myself and
Mr. Ryan are starving. I find the babies very
expensive to feed, they have got very big. I am
not well. I told the nurse in the clinic how I feel,
and she said I am not getting enough food, I am
bleeding and not getting enough rest. The babies
are a terrible handful, and I will not have the
energy to travel. I feel very sick indeed, so could
you please try to arrange some place for me here in
England? I would be more than grateful. Please do
something soon, as if I do get really very ill, they*

will really have to be taken then. I love the babies.
If I could I would keep them, but I have nothing
for them, to keep them with. They will know who
I am soon, and it will be harder on me and them if
they are not adopted soon.

The acknowledgment of how hard this was going to be on all of them was especially poignant and prophetic. I was so saddened to read the sorrow and heartache in those letters from 1958, which remained hidden for the rest of her life. There was no prospect for the babies and surely, we would have died of malnutrition, tuberculosis or any number of childhood diseases at the time. The wrong timing would have put us in one of the mother baby homes where infants disappeared.

My mother did all that she could, and as the story of her life was pieced together through letters and conversations with relatives, it felt to me like the grayness of that first ferry ride to London must've soaked into her soul and never left.

She deserved to know that her children had survived, that we were looking for her. That imagined reunion still haunts me. A simple act of charity by The Sisters of Charity would have reassured my mother that all she sacrificed had given us a life beyond the confines of stone institutions designed to weigh down fallen children with punishments for sins they did not commit.

The 2014 administrators of Saint Patrick's Guild and their predecessors shut the door on my mother when she needed God the most; condemning her to be needlessly crucified by condemnations. The law of the Eucharist in the Catholic Canon states: those who are "obstinately persevering in manifest grave sin are not to be admitted to Holy Communion" (No. 915).

For many, like Sister Edith, this was interpreted as meaning there is no redemption for adulteresses. They are to be cast out as if they are Satan's minions, along with their children. This attitude was pervasive when I was born.

The Sixth Century sermon by Pope Gregory the Great calling Mary Magdalene a fallen woman was a condemnation of all women who sin and shut the door to transubstantiation during the Eucharist. The world had to be cleansed of such sinners and their spawn, and the Catholic Church led the charge.

Sister Edith was only too happy to be a soldier in the war. She reveled in the pain my mother suffered as if it was somehow a holy process of separating the wheat from the tares. I had to wonder how the scene of Jesus forgiving the woman caught in adultery had escaped them. Could they not see that they were exactly as the Pharisees casting stones?

The Crusade of Rescue summary and Betty's letters confirmed that Patrick Ryan was our father. We discovered that Patrick had stayed to help Betty in London, through the delivery of the twins and through the first four months. We also discovered another significant clue; Patrick was the father of two sons back in Ireland; I wondered if they would be as accepting as Betty's family.

CHAPTER

Twenty-Two

Susan Googled the 1911 address listed in the Irish Census; the flat on Upper Dorset where the Cleary family had lived. She found a link to the blog of an Australian, Phil Cleary. Email communication ensued and they determined that Phil and I shared a common second great grandfather. Phil's great grandfather had emigrated to Australia while Daniel Cleary, my great grandfather had left County Limerick for Dublin in the late 1890s. On his blog, Phil Cleary had a photo of Betty's sister Joan Cleary, photos of the Upper Dorset property, and stories of my great aunts, Nellie, and Marie Cleary.

Phil had written about the association of the Dublin Cleary family with the Republican cause and the civil war of Ireland that occurred after the revolution. The Cleary's had been staunchly anti-treaty. Phil had quoted Aunt Joan in his writing, regarding the Cleary family Republican involvement. IRA leader Michael Collins used to operate from the Cleary cooperage safehouse, and Marie had been scouting for him on the morning of the Easter Rebellion. Maybe I should get that tattoo after all. I love a good rebellion.

Here were direct relatives that stood up and fought for a just cause. Emboldened by the discovery I wanted to go back to Sacred Heart where I began my education and confront the nuns who had paddled me. My family tree was branching out and my roots were growing stronger. The stories and photos from Phil were a treasure.

In a subsequent email, Phil said that, in preparation for his writing, he had been in contact with a woman that would be my first cousin, a Noreen Cleary. A first cousin, with the surname Cleary, could only be a daughter of one of Betty's two brothers. Tony had indicated that Liam Cleary, Betty's younger brother had been married, but had never had children. The only other brother was Donal. Could Noreen Cleary be one of the lost daughters that were sent to Goldenbridge Orphanage after Donal's death? Phil provided us an email address that summer and we wrote immediately to Noreen. Noreen and her husband Philip responded. Noreen was indeed one of Donal's lost daughters. She had survived.

We immediately emailed Tony to tell him that we had located Noreen, Donal's daughter. Noreen and her older sisters had indeed been taken and placed in Goldenbridge Orphanage for months, due to the same societal and Irish Catholic Church rule; destroying families who didn't conform. The little girls had a terrible time of it. The older girls (age 9 and 6) were required to work for their keep doing laundry and stringing rosaries. Noreen, only 4 wouldn't have been old enough to be put to work for 2 more years.

Betty would not have known of Mary, Noreen's mother, and her situation. But she would have known of the Magdalene laundries. Reading my mother's letters, you could sense her deep fear for her children. And here, in another branch of the family, that fear had been realized. I have no account of what happened to the girls while they were in the Goldenbridge Orphanage, but there are accounts of children being flogged and starved in the medieval prison that was Goldenbridge.

May Henderson was incarcerated at Goldenbridge at the age of 2 at about the same time Noreen and her sisters would have been there. May was taken forcefully from her mother for being illegitimate. She remained there for 15 years despite the pleadings of her father that he could take care of her. The nuns refused any contact, and even hid 31 letters he wrote to her while he was serving in the military. She finally received the letters at age 70. From the time May entered Goldenbridge to the time she left as a teenager, her life was hell. She was left to sleep in her own urine when she wet the bed, which would most certainly be a result of trauma. She was beaten often for minor transgressions, whipped with rosary beads and even had her teeth knocked out that resulted in her being hospitalized. Apparently one of the nuns was an expert at flagellation. "She would beat you with rosary beads while she prayed and you recited the Hail Mary," May recounted in an interview with the Guardian. "The sick thing about it was that we, the children, made those rosary beads in the workshop, which were sold to convents, holy shops and parishes."

May's testimony became known because she was protesting the LaFoy Commission, a directive to investigate child abuse. "When the LaFoy Commission was first established I wrote to them and told my story," she said. "They recommended that I should get some counseling to come to terms with what went on in Goldenbridge."

"They recommended that I speak to the Immigrant Counseling and Psychotherapy group at Islington, London."

"It was only when I went there that I found out that the centre is run by a Sister Teresa Gallagher of the Loretto Convent and member of the Conference of Religious in Ireland. The Irish government funds it."

Imagine after finally finding the courage to deal with the abuse by nuns and your reward is being assigned a nun as a therapist."

Luckily, Mary, Noreen's strong and courageous mother, was eventually successful in getting her daughters out of Goldenbridge. How she did it remains unclear, but it seems miraculous to me.

Tony and Maura were delighted that Noreen and her sisters had been found. Noreen, Philip, Tony and Maura, and their families were able to connect nearly seven decades after having been separated. Some branches of family trees are lopped off and hopefully we can graft them back in. Philip and Noreen had spent years researching their family histories, including Noreen's paternal side. They shared with us the large body of research that corroborated and enhanced the research we had done on the common ancestors. It was a treasure to find these dear cousins.

Two months after having found Noreen, the documentary, "Ireland's Lost Babies" aired in Ireland and the UK. In it, I had shared the photo of Betty that I received from Maura and Tony, just before filming.

The evening the program aired, an elderly widow, by the name of Rose decided that she didn't want to watch, as the programs regarding adoption of children to the US always made her sad. Her daughter was visiting at the time and helped Rose record the program in case she wanted to watch it later. Such is the pervasiveness of sorrow in so many Irish families.

The next day Rose decided to watch the recorded program. The documentary ended up being a compilation of several universally sad stories of adopted Irish babies and birth mothers. As Rose watched the story of a man adopted from Ireland to California, the program zoomed in on a photo of the man's birth mother. The photo was of Rose's first cousin Betty Mancell!

Rose immediately called her daughter to tell her of the shock and sadness she had just experienced, seeing Betty's photo, as the mother of a man in California who had been looking for her for all these years.

Rose's daughter had a connection with a person who worked for the BBC and eventually was connected through them to me. Technology changed everything about genealogical research. I began communicating with Rose's daughter and shared photos, including a photo of Betty's wedding day of a group of people outside the Synge Street front door. Rose was a darling 16-year-old in the photo! In her first email she wrote:

Hello Michael and Susan and all your gorgeous family,

I am delighted to be in contact with you. You were a hard man to contact but my daughter managed through the BBC. You have sent me so much material, (Some of which I never saw before) you will have to give me time to get my breath back! My use of the computer is pathetic, but I manage the email... You

*seem to have your mother's dimples. I regret that
I wouldn't have any information on your birth
and adoption, but I will have family background
information. Will be in touch soon again.*

*I am your first cousin once removed,
Rose.*

I responded:

Hello Rose,

*Thank you so much for your kind words. Delighted
to have passed on Betty's dimples to my son
Christopher! Looking forward to hearing family
background information,*

*Warmest regards,
Michael.*

I began to function as facilitator, connecting first
cousins and second cousins once removed, filling in the
family tree on my mother's side. Soon, this family that had
been estranged for so long, began to communicate with each
other, take long drives in the country and search through
cemeteries. I remembered a scripture in Isaiah: *"The hearts
of the children will be turned to their fathers."* It was prophetic.

Despite the obstacles of the last sixty years, here was
a family coming together. I had to smile at the wonder of
it all. Still, while the relatives found joy with each new
connection, our work had not yet turned up the one person
I now wanted most to discover: my father.

CHAPTER

Twenty-Three

he search for Patrick Ryan was like looking for a needle among a pile of needles. The Census records that included a Patrick Ryan, between the age of 2-4 in 1911 were over 100. There was no way to narrow down the Census data to find the Patrick Ryan that belonged to me and my sister.

On June 19, 2015, on a whim, Susan searched public trees on Ancestry.com for trees with a Patrick Ryan, born 1907-1909. There were seven matching Patrick Ryan's in the entire database. We sent the following Ancestry.com message to all seven tree owners:

Hi,

I am searching for my Irish family. My father was Patrick Ryan, a musician who also worked on the railroad in the UK in the 1950s and 1960s.

Regards,
Michael

Only one of the tree owners responded. He replied the next day:

Hello Michael,

I had an uncle who lived his latter life in Luton, Beds. He did play the clarinet in a showband in Ireland during early life. Though his main employment was in Vauxhalls as a car sprayer. Of course, there could be some distant relationship. Look at my tree if you wish.

Good luck in your searches.
Noel

I tried to tamp down my excitement. We had followed so many dead ends. Yet this was promising.

I replied quickly.

Hello Noel,

Thank you for your reply. The Patrick I am searching for was listed as an auto mechanic. I have a document that lists his place of residence at 3 Willow Court, Leagrave, Luton in October 1960. He may have lived temporarily at 15 Leinster Square W.2 Bayswater. An additional document states that he was the father of 2 sons as of 1958. An additional document states that he was an occasional musician in a Dublin establishment—although not his profession—as late as 1955.

*My search is rather sensitive, as the Patrick Ryan I
am researching met my mother in an establishment
in Dublin in 1955 which was the beginning of a
relationship, which eventually led to my conception.
I also have a twin sister. We were born to our Irish
mother in April 1958. According to letters furnished
by the Catholic Children's Society Crusade of Rescue,
our mother kept us in London at the Leinster
Square residence with Patrick Ryan until we
were 4 months, at which time, our mother took us
back to Dublin to relinquish us for adoption. We
were in orphanages until the age of 3 1/2. We have
a document from the solicitors Currall and Randall
of Luton regarding Patrick Ryan's acknowledgement
that we were his children and that he had no
objection to our adoption. We were adopted to the
United States in 1961. I began looking for our birth
mother in 1995 but was thwarted by the adoption
society until we received notification four months
after our mother's death in 1997.*

*Is there a possibility that the Patrick Ryan we are
searching for is your uncle?*

*Regards,
Michael*

*P.S. Just for a bit of authentication, The BBC
programme "This World" learned of our adoption
search story and we were part of a documentary
last fall that aired in the UK and Ireland. It was
called Ireland's Lost Babies.*

*The following is a link to an article regarding the
BBC documentary with Martin Sixsmith who
interviewed me in California and in Dublin, regarding
our adoption search. The photo of the two toddlers
with the nun on the steps of the orphanage are of me
and my sister. The documentary may still be available
in the UK. Can't seem to get it here anymore.*

Regards, Michael."

The Guardian reviewed the documentary and had this
to say:

"There's no point, really, in even trying to prepare
yourself mentally or emotionally for a programme
entitled This World: Ireland's Lost Babies
(BBC2). The bald facts, laid out by presenter
Martin Sixsmith as he made his way between
the emerald isle and the US, were bad enough.
Between 40,000 and 60,000 babies were—by legal
standards today and moral standards any time—
involuntarily given up for adoption in the 1950s
and 60s by Roman Catholic Irishwomen who
became pregnant outside marriage. The treatment
of the "fallen women" at the mother and baby
homes run by fiercely unforgiving nuns was
appalling. The vetting procedures for potential
adoptive parents were worse. Catholic? Moneyed?
You're in. Take your pick.

"It didn't matter, as Mike Hawkes and his twin
sister found out, if you were the brother of a

paedophile priest who would rule your family with a rod of iron. 'Going against his will was not healthy. Not healthy at all."

To be clear, I didn't set out to shame the Catholic Church, only to hold them accountable and to find my origins and connect with whatever family members I could. Mine is a David and Goliath story, one that I never would have embarked on if it were not for Susan. Squinting at a flickering computer screen into the wee hours, Susan found crumbs and clues, made contacts, and corresponded. This latest correspondence felt promising.

Noel replied:

Hi Michael,

I Cannot confirm, my uncle Patrick is the same one, (your father). I have no information about his life in London whatsoever. I do know he had two sons and lived in Luton, Bedfordshire up until his death in September 1989. He had several employers one, Buckley's Motors in Dublin, Vauxhall motors as a paint finisher in Luton. Last address was 55 Puckeridge Road, Luton. He lived in Willow Way, Luton twice.

What was the maiden name of your Mother? This might help.

Noel

To which I replied:

Our mother's maiden name was Elizabeth Esther Cleary. She was known as Betty. Her married name was Mancell, having married a man from Wales. She was estranged from her husband within months of her marriage in 1949 and left to live with her mother on Synge Street in Dublin. It was apparently in that neighborhood where she was working as a waitress at the establishment where Patrick was playing in the band on occasion. They apparently had a long-term relationship, prior to our birth.

While in Dublin we also made a visit to the adoption agency, and we were given the document listing the name and Luton, Willow Way, address of Patrick Ryan. The document was from his solicitor in Luton. Until then we did not have his name or any information other than the misinformation about his age that we were given from St. Patrick's Guild.

Would be grateful for any direction you can give us as to the continuation of our search to confirm that we have found the correct Patrick Ryan.

It had been an extraordinarily bold inquiry and much to ask of Noel. However, considering the congruent details about his uncle's 1960 residence, musician in a Dublin establishment, matching name, age, profession, etc., Noel's curiosity was piqued. He had been convinced that it was a possibility that his Patrick Ryan was my birth Father, Patrick Ryan. Noel began to investigate. This, to me, was quite courageous. What ghosts from the past would he uncover that might shake his family tree?

Armed with the information that I had shared of my adoption and search journey, Noel approached Annette, the daughter of Patrick's son, Barney. Annette shared the story with her mother Anne. Anne approached Barney, saying, "Do you recall your father having a friend by the name of Betty in Dublin?"

The next communication came by email. Noel wrote:

Hi, Susan & Michael

I have made several inquiries about my Patrick Ryan, although it's not conclusive, without documentation, I feel it is extremely likely that he was the father you're looking for. I did in fact remember him as a brother of my mother, Mary Clare Fanning nee Ryan.

I'm sure as I suggested you will have looked at my family tree on Ancestry.UK. And concluded that he had two sons, Gerard & Bernard.

Unfortunately, Gerry passed away in 2011. Bernard (Barney) is alive and well living in Luton. I spoke to him this morning and he has no recollection of any of this. I felt uneasy revealing your story, but he was fine about it. I guess this makes us cousins then. I'm sure you will have further information and may require more from me, do let me know.

Noel Fanning

It was an uncomfortable and difficult inquiry, sharing the possibility that Barney's father, Patrick, had been unfaithful to Barney's mother in 1957, resulting in the conception of twin half siblings. Barney, Anne, and the Ryan family looked at the very convincing paper trail we sent, including the letter from the Luton solicitors, and concluded that Barney had two more siblings who had been living in America.

We booked dates for Dublin and would travel to England to meet Noel, Barney, and the Ryan family.

The first photo of Patrick Ryan was received by Susan in the wee hours one morning. The eight-hour time difference between England and California resulted in emails being sent from England, while the California residents were asleep. Susan woke at 5am to find that Noel had sent a photo. She excitedly tried to wake me and said, "Would you like to see a photo of your father?"

Half asleep, I looked at Susan and said, "Would he look the same after all these years at say seven am?"

Then on second thought, fearing for my safety, given the work Susan had put into finding Patrick Ryan, I rolled out of bed to take a look. There on the iPad screen was a well-dressed older gentleman. Susan had found him.

"He was a good-looking chap!" I said.

Once again, the mild-mannered RN had proved herself a tenacious sleuth. I lay awake waiting for the sunlight to fill the room, half afraid that if I fell back asleep the whole thing would have been a dream.

It was one thing to be raised by a man who portrayed himself as your father in public and privately despised you. Now knowing my blood father would open up questions that could not be answered: would he have been just as abusive? Would he have resented us? Could he have adopted us? Did I actually have a better life—despite the abuse—having been raised in America? I leaned on the affection I'd experienced from the relatives on my mother's side for strength. The pattern of self-doubts inflicted on me by my adoptive father and the shame I experienced at the hands of my uncle were still deep.

It takes a strong will to face life head-on and change deep-seated emotional responses. My mother's courage had been with me all along, I realized. Whatever I found out about my father, the truth would be more satisfactory than the uncertainty.

CHAPTER

Twenty-Four

We flew from Los Angeles directly to Heathrow, three months after having found Noel Fanning's family tree; three months after taking the wild chance that a tree owner would respond to such a message.

Annette and John, Barney's kids would pick us up at the airport. I wondered how the meeting with the Ryan side of the family would go. We felt such a connection to my mother's side that I was both wildly optimistic, and quietly uncertain. So far, all conversations had been positive.

On the flight over I continued to ponder the great implications of my sudden appearance in the family. Imagine someone knocking on your door and saying, "I'm your long-lost brother! Your father had an affair, and I was secretly shipped off to America. How about a hug"!

Barney and I shared the same father, but not the same mother. What do you say to each other in this situation? "I would have called sooner but there were these evil nuns and lost papers and my mother died but I'm here now!"

I gazed out over the ocean and fretted over every word I would say, anticipating their reaction. I also wondered if I was being selfish by invading this family's world, changing the family narrative.

By the time we exited the plane a knot had formed in my stomach. My usual defense mechanism of using humor to evade intense emotions had left me. I was dead silent as we made the long walk down the concourse and hallways of Heathrow airport to the gathering area.

I seriously imagined a crowd of people with pitchforks and signs that read: "Go back to America!" But outside the baggage claim, my eyes fell to two people we recognized from Facebook, John, and Annette, both waving. Annette gave us a big hug.

There was that brief, awkward pause that happens when you are not quite sure how to greet somebody in a foreign country. I reached out my hand and was pulled into an embrace. They couldn't have been more welcoming.

While walking through the parking lot, John turned left then right swearing he knew exactly where he had left his car to take us on the fifty-minute journey to Luton.

As any sister would do, Annette ripped him humorously saying, "Here we are again; John is lost!"

It was funny and broke the ice. But more importantly, was a signal that there would be no pretenses, no putting on appearances—something I had become highly attuned to in my younger years. I loved them immediately.

The car was found, and we were off. I was grateful that I wasn't driving on the wrong side of the road and navigating this major London area motorway. As we drove, the family had a lot of questions as you can imagine. We shared what we knew so far of Betty's life and family. John and Annette were saddened by what Betty had to endure. I reassured them that Patrick had done all he could.

"Times are different now," Annette said.

John was more pensive. "All those Irish babies. What became of them?"

I was lost in thought. It did seem like we were going back in time over a hundred years, exploring a social structure from the dark ages. I can only imagine how difficult this journey was for Patrick's family. Patrick was well loved, a good provider. He never lost himself in drink and always took his responsibilities seriously as a father.

The Irish are a passionate people, particularly when it comes to clans. Patrick must have felt the dishonor that would befall the family if his two illegitimate children were ever found out.

On that drive, while I learned more about Patrick, Susan sat in the back with Annette and unfolded our story. By the time we arrived in Luton town, John and Annette had the synopsis of the twenty-year search for my heritage and family.

I continued to worry about what I was going to say to Barney. Talking has always been a kind of self-defense for me: joking, holding conversations, steering them away from hard emotions. This entire trip required me to face awkward and difficult situations. I wasn't good at it. And I worried incessantly about it.

As we drove through picturesque Luton, John and Annette pointed out Vauxhall, the factory that made automobiles. This was where Patrick Ryan worked. It left me with a lump in my throat. Past the factory and up hills was a residential area. English connected homes covered the landscape. It was like driving along Privet Drive in Harry Potter. In some ways I felt like Jim Carrey in The Truman Show. All that I had been living had been constructed for me and I was about to step into my real life.

We pulled up to a very pleasant housing community of clean white homes. I was still on edge. Car doors opened and we walked slowly out onto a path to the front of the home. John opened the door and immediately a very lovely Irish lady was introduced to us; it was Anne, Barney's wife, mother of Annette, John, and Kevin. She was first introduced to Susan. She and Susan embraced immediately.

Anne had a lovely smile and a warm countenance. My heartbeat slowed down. In my peripheral vision, I saw a man approach from a side room. He was older than me by seventeen years. He was of medium build, eyes that twinkled, with a fine head of gray hair. The man immediately walked up to me put his hand out to his newfound brother and said, "Welcome Michael and Susan!"

It was such a warm handshake.

"Three years ago," he continued, "I lost a brother to cancer—our brother—Gerry. Now I find that I have another brother and a sister!"

I was stunned with the kind welcome. I was home. Barney had made peace with the sensitive nature of the news that he had a half brother and sister. It's hard to describe the spiritual nature of the meeting. It was as if God said, "You all are family. You are connected forever."

The dreamscape of Ireland is so rich in romantic images and history, the people so real compared to the California existence I grew up in, that I had to sit for a moment, let a few tears fall and just breathe it all in. Susan held onto my arm and could sense the release of so many emotions.

My childhood was one of punishment, abuse, and confinement. My working years had been clouded by uncertainty, even as we had children and bonded so tightly with our little family. But in the corners of my heart, beside the pain of my childhood there was a longing. And in that embrace, it was evaporated into that rare Irish sun.

More family members came by, daughters and sons, aunts and cousins, including many of Anne's family, the Dohertys. They had all seen the BBC program "Ireland's Lost Babies" and were moved to tears. To have one returned was as emotional for them as it was for me.

A little later in the evening a knock at the door and in entered Noel Fanning. We greeted Noel and expressed our gratitude that he made his Ancestry.com tree public and had taken the bold leap to share my story of the search for Patrick Ryan.

Barney looks the part of the Irish host—the beaming smile and sparkling eyes that belie his 75 years. He was up early the next morning and school was on. We had a lot to learn about the family, a lot to see, and a lot to feel. We toured Luton and visited the grave of our father Patrick, buried next to Barney's mother. We visited the grave of our brother, Gerry. I was surprised at how the sadness fell on me. A half-brother I had never met, yet I sorrowed at his passing.

Barney turned to me and said, "I wish you could've met our brother Gerry. I'll have to do. You're my brother, I won't say 'Half-brother.'"

Barney took us all over Luton town, introducing me, as his long-lost brother, to his friends. Some of the people we met had heard from Barney about his newfound American brother. Many had watched "Ireland's Lost Babies" and expressed their heart-felt condolences for my difficulties with the Catholic Church run St. Patrick's Guild.

And of course, in that ancient Irish tradition, we had a large family gathering at a pub: O'Shea's, a Ryan family favorite. John and his wife Liane warned us to be prepared for the nephews, nieces, and cousins onslaught, as they all had heard the story of the lost Irish American twins. O'Shea's began filling up. I have no idea how many people I met. I was overwhelmed with gratitude that this large, closely knit, salt of the earth family had accepted my sister and I as their own.

We were delighted to meet the dear family of my brother Gerry as well as Barney and Anne's family. Glasses were raised with the phrase slainte! I imagined that in some way it was like dying and going to heaven, being greeted by all those who had gone before, the long and broad net of ancestors who love you. Little Michael Anthony Mancell, native son, returned after 55 years banished.

The next day we took the train ride from Luton to London. In my guarded childhood imagination, I had always envisioned my mother living in a castle set in the rolling green hills of Ireland. Retracing her steps and painful life settled on me. In the midst of so much affection and generosity, I hoped she was watching, her soft face lit with satisfaction and her kind eyes finally gazing down on the reunion she had so long prayed for.

CHAPTER

Twenty-Five

Storytellers and secret keepers. To such belongs the family history. I thought about a grapevine in Bill's yard. One of the vines had grown through the fence. We didn't discover it until I was cleaning up the pruning in the fall. The vine had grown unnoticed and had a nice cluster of grapes. It had been hidden for a season, and then discovered. The lost branches of my family tree were found.

Barney booked a flight to Dublin a few days into the trip, to show us *his* Dublin and the family neighborhoods. I was anxious to know more about my father, about the family life he cultivated. There were Ryan's who had not left Ireland, first cousins. They had planned to meet us as well. We were now well out on the Ryan branch of the family tree. We were invited to the home of another Dublin Ryan and family, descendants of my late Uncle Michael. All the cousins and extended family gathered to meet us and hear my story. The Ryan's in Dublin were just as welcoming as Barney and the clan in Luton.

Barney took us on a walking tour of his old neighborhoods. We saw the cottages in which Patrick

Ryan had been raised and in which he and his wife had raised Barney and Gerry, before moving to Luton.

We walked the canal where young Barney and Gerry had fished, instead of attending the music lessons Patrick had arranged for them. I could see myself beside them, the younger brother nosing his way into their activities and trailing behind. It made me smile.

When I heard of Barney's great escapades and the successful dodging of the nuns and authorities in his youth, the blood bond was sealed. Yes, we were brothers. I reckoned we would've gotten on like a house on fire.

We stood on one of the canal bridges where Barney had carved "BR" in the stone. It was still visible. In a moment of sentimentality, it came to me that our brotherhood was equally carved in stone. Barney offered an apology for not knowing of my situation when I was taken from my home in Ireland. For a moment I wanted to carve my initials next to his. "It's now we have," I said. "Patrick would be happy."

Our next stop was at the cemetery with more family members: Rose, Noreen, and Philip. We had spent months corresponding by email, sharing genealogical research, family lore, photos, and plans. Noreen drove us around Dublin, past the Synge Street home. Noreen's mother was buried very near the grave of Lizzie, Betty, Joan and Eilish. After so many years without a stone there was now a marker that named her children, and a phrase I asked Tony to add: "Families are Forever," the same sentiment written on the grave of our son Nicholas.

The day before we were to fly home, Rose had planned for a tour of historical Glasnevin Cemetery. Many of my ancestors were buried there. Rose led the little band of researchers to the graves of those she had found, many adorned with the Celtic cross. I've thought often of the Celtic cross since my first trip to Ireland. The circle that overlays the center of the cross feels to me like all things not only come back to where they started, but circle around God. It's a perfect symbol of our journey, each of us searching for God in our own way, searching for our origins, circling back to ancestors with God at the center of our odyssey.

Philip, an avid genealogical researcher, said to Susan: "I had a very vivid dream, in which the Old Ones came to me and told me they wanted me to find them." It reminded me of the genealogy poem whose author is unknown,

> *"We are the chosen.*
>
> *In each family, there is one who seems called to find the ancestors.*
>
> *To put flesh on their bones and make them live again,*
>
> *to tell the family story and to feel that somehow, they know and approve.*
>
> *Doing genealogy is not a cold gathering of facts, but instead,*
>
> *breathing life into all who have gone before.*
>
> *We are the storytellers of the tribe."*

We count ourselves extremely fortunate to have found our storytellers, Noel, the Ryan family genealogist, and Philip the Cleary family genealogist.

CHAPTER

Twenty-Six

In the coming months, a DNA aspect emerged in our search. I had completed testing on several sites, before we found the convincing paper trail that would eventually lead to finding Tony, and long before we found Noel and Barney. Noel had his DNA tested just before Susan and I left during the last trip. Results returned that Noel was indeed my first cousin. Multiple 2nd, 3rd and 4th cousin matches began to emerge, as DNA testing had become extremely popular and more readily available outside of the US.

We had matches to cousins who were the children and grandchildren of Daniel and Honoria Cleary, Daniel's parents and Honoria's parents, and Betty's maternal lines. The DNA matches hailed from Ireland, England, Canada, the USA, and Australia, all the places our Irish forebearers' descendants had emigrated to, mostly because of the Irish famine.

A second cousin, Dermot from Australia, was able to share a large document of his years of research on the paternal lines of Betty. From papers left by his late mother, Dermot was able to share many photos, including a beautiful portrait of Honoria, Betty's grandmother. We shared this with Rose, Noreen, Philip, and all the other DNA match descendants of Honoria. No one, outside of Dermot, had a copy of this photo.

On subsequent trips back and forth to England and Ireland, we were always pleased to visit with family members we had already met. On another trip to Luton, we met Kevin, Barney and Anne's son from Perth, his wife Nicola and their two darling girls. Kevin and I went out to the local golf club for the first annual Ryan Ryder cup golf tournament between Kevin and me. I, the senior of the two golfers "let" my newfound nephew take the trophy, after all, family is more important than winning. Well, that's the best I could come up with after the sound thrashing on the links. While I was golfing, Susan was taken to an afternoon tea at the Luton Hoo, with all the ladies.

In 2017, we were accompanied by all four of our adult children and four grandchildren and Susan's mother back to Ireland and England. Susan and I watched with great contentment as our children and grandchildren interacted with Beatty, Cleary and Ryan aunts, uncles, and cousins for the first time. The highlight of the trip was a Ryan family party thrown by Barney and his family at the Luton Celtic Club. It was a joy to have the Hawkes children and grandchildren cherished and welcomed by the maternal and paternal family. And so, the Cleary, Ryan family tree branched out even more.

CHAPTER

Twenty-Seven

*I*t takes time and plenty of questions to gain the altitude necessary to see your life clearly. Each family connection elevates. So much of what I experienced in my early life was sequestered away behind doors marked "Do Not Touch."

The PTSD that resulted made it difficult to see clearly. Meeting Susan caused some of the scales to fall from my eyes. Having children sharpened my vision. And finally, connecting with family across generations and the boughs of relationships brought into focus my life in a way that I could not have accomplished on my own.

I believe the first part of my life to be managed by man, the latter half with all it's wonder and healing, to be orchestrated by God. I had to climb to that point in order to write it all down.

So much of life for thousands of years has been simple survival. The meaning of existence was pondered by the few elites in Greek culture and religious teachings across all cultures. What strikes me is the tapestry of beliefs that made surviving life bearable. This endless search to know who we are, where we came from, where we are headed has created great societies. I believe there is divinity in each effort to gain knowledge.

As we search, we each go through our own personal enlightenment, an awakening. We discover God. My life is proof that He is there and I hope that what I have experienced gives shape to the being that created us.

At the same time, throughout history there have been those who shaped God into their own image. I believe that leaders in the Catholic Church took upon themselves the responsibilities of God and exploited a vulnerable population they had sworn to protect. In a twisted sense of righteousness, we were purged from their sight.

It was well understood and documented that the Catholic Church in the 1950s and beyond, along with the blessing of the government of Ireland. ordered and directed people's lives in a very corrupt and destructive manner. Countless times Susan and I were told that the search for my family origins would come to an unsatisfying end, that we should end the search, not disrupt lives. To deprive one of divine connections is perhaps the greatest evil after abusing innocents. Or maybe the greater sin is covering it all up.

The goal of the Irish government and the Catholic Church, I believe, was to prevent these stolen children and disrupted families the restitution of reconnection. The Church and the government should be exposed for the frauds that I believe they are in their history of ruining the lives of so many. It seems that any gang or mafia type organization working in a sinister manner to profit in the human trade business, or "trafficking," would be prosecuted for criminal activity. The diversions and deceptive manipulations used as a way to throw people off their search are unfathomable to me even now.

On March 9, 2017, a prominent leader of the Irish government summed it up better than we could possibly try to do. Taoiseach leader Enda Kenny spoke these words,

> *...No nuns broke into our homes to kidnap our children. We gave them up to what we convinced ourselves was the nuns' care. We gave them up maybe to spare them the savagery of gossip, the wink, and the elbow language of delight in which the holier than thous were particularly fluent. We gave them up because of our perverse, in fact, morbid relationship with what is called respectability. Indeed, for a while it seemed as if in Ireland our women had the amazing capacity to self-impregnate. For their trouble, we took their babies and gifted them, sold them, trafficked them, starved them, neglected them, or denied them to the point of their disappearance from our hearts, our sight, our country and, in the case of Tuam and possibly other places, from life itself.*

> *We are all shocked now. If the fruit of her religious and social transgression could be discarded, what treatment was meted out to the transgressor herself? We better deal with this now because if we do not, some other Taoiseach will be standing here in 20 years saying, "If only we knew then and if only we had done then."*

This Taoiseach—Irish for Prime Minister—was speaking on behalf of the Irish government of the day to address the horrors of years of social and cultural abuse.

So, the church and the government colluded for decades to "do the best that they knew how." I was tired of hearing those words. Those were the words used by Sister Edith to describe that the orphanage did "the best they knew how" when handing children over to families for a pre-arranged sale price. No, they did not do the best they knew how; what they did I believe was the best they knew to protect the Church and for profit over and over again in human trafficking.

Susan and I fought and fought to find and turn over any stone to find my mother, father, and brothers. The Church and the State had absolutely no right after all those years of hiding my mother from me to then decide to hide my father away from me in a dark closet behind lock and key. I am reminded of a quote by Martin Luther King:

Shallow understanding from people of good will

is more frustrating than absolute misunderstanding from people of ill will.

These efforts from St Patrick's Guild were not only the work of people with "shallow understanding," but also evil well-planned conniving "people of ill will." Here were religious leaders and Parliament high-minded officials scheming, writing, and setting policy for Ireland.

The reign of terror from the Church and government policies also stretched into England, the United States, Scotland, Spain, Australia and beyond.

The magnitude of the abuse is still being uncovered. Many children were illegally adopted out in Ireland. Many after the practice was made illegal. Sexual abuse numbers are difficult to come by. Based on criminal charges somewhere between 3,000 and 4,500 priests and deacons are accused of sexually molesting young boys between 1950 and 2004.

I know Pope John Paul ll apologized for sexual abuse in the church in 2001 calling it "a profound contradiction of the teachings of the witnesses of Jesus Christ," in June of 2021. But the U.N. special reporters for the Office of the High Commissioner for Human Rights criticized the Vatican and presented continued allegations that the Catholic Church had failed in their oversight of priests and to cooperate with domestic judicial proceedings.

The report expressed. "*Utmost concern about the numerous allegations around the world of sexual abuse and violence committed by members of the Catholic Church against children, and about the measures adopted by the Catholic Church to protect alleged abusers, cover up crimes, obstruct accountability of alleged abusers, and evade reparations due to victims.*" They also noted "*the persistent allegations of obstruction and lack of cooperation by the Catholic Church with domestic legal proceedings to prevent accountability of perpetrators and reparations to victims.*

I was 37 when I began my search. The Catholic Church knew then where my mother was. St Patrick's Guild officials knew where she was. I could have had a few years of correspondence, visits, Christmas cards and Mother's Day calls. What harm would it have done the Church to reunite mother and child? Obviously, my mother knew nothing of what happened to her twins, and she should not have passed with that weight on her mind. Had we been given the 1960 letter from my father's solicitor in 1996, we may have met my maternal sister and both of my paternal brothers.

The pious religious orders wanted nothing to do with reunions and restitution. When Susan questioned Sister Edith's stonewalling our efforts to bring some comfort to my mother, her only response was: "She had her faith, and that was enough."

Then she released the info we had been asking for. The closest I came to touching my mother was at her grave.

Bill and Helen, my adopted parents spoke these words to me years after leaving home and visiting them with Susan and two young children, "We did the best we knew how." It was a cold statement, self-justification even, as Bill knew that his brother had molested me.

The best you know how is not to continue to send a young boy to a pedophile on the weekends, or to whip him into submission.

Perhaps they considered two Irish orphans as short-term projects, or a way to gain status by their supposed generosity. I don't know, I don't understand, but I do know that my story could not have happened without their part; a story that led me to a place that perhaps I wouldn't have gotten to if I had been raised in Dublin. I never told them about my search for my biological parents, it was a journey that belonged to me; not to be shared with them.

I did eventually return to Ireland with my twin sister. In 2017, we re-stepped the journey together, starting at the red door of the Catholic Protection Society of Ireland, and finishing at Betty's grave. She was embraced just as I was by the family. Barney was especially happy. He embraced my sister, our sister, with such tenderness. "I always wanted a sister," he said.

As Bill and Helen aged, and their lives shortened before them, I would fly from Los Angeles to Northern

California to visit with them as often as time would permit. After Helen passed, Bill grew sad. Our talks in those last years of his life were always about how much he missed his wife. They did everything together and he loved her deeply.

It was on a Sunday when my phone rang and on the other end of the line was my older sister. We didn't say much in those years, but she had been visiting Bill and told me: "Dad asked where you were. I told him you lived in Los Angeles."

Bill was slipping away. I pondered his life, at least what I knew of it. The conversation with my older sister was pleasant; we talked for a few minutes before hanging up. She called again the next night. "Michael, he's asking about you again. Can you come up?"

"I'll see what I can do." It was Monday night. I quickly found a flight out the next morning. I honestly was unclear as to why he was so keen on seeing me. But I had a gut feeling that I needed to be there. The next afternoon my plane landed in San Jose, and I called from the car. "How is he?"

"He's weak, but this morning he asked about you."

I travelled the freeway and roads I knew so well. I pulled onto his street and rolled past the Chrisman's. I parked the car in the long driveway. As I walked to the front door, memories and emotions flooded back to me—good and bad. My family life was a dichotomy, a collision of wanting to belong and wanting to leave, of wanting to give affection and wanting to withhold. How was this final meeting between me and my adoptive father going to go? I knocked and the hospice care giver opened the door. I introduced myself.

"Yes," she said. "Michael. I've heard about you."

I was ushered into the room where Bill lay on his deathbed knowing it would be the last time I would ever be in this house. Having contemplated the question *what is a normal father and son relationship supposed to look like?* I concluded a father, in some ways, should be a hero, a loving example, a strong individual who teams up with mother and forms an unbreakable bond as a family that nothing in the world can distort or tear apart.

I had never heard the words "I love you" from Bill or Helen. Nor had I ever expressed my love for them. Here Bill lay dying and I was searching the depths of my existence for those words.

In his bed covered in a blanket was a frail 98-year-old man. I stood above him and stared out the window, looking at the grounds of the backyard. I recalled as a boy Bill getting up early on Saturday mornings to work in the yard he loved so much, tending to the Rose Garden and to the fruit trees. Bill always brought me outside with him to work, spreading fertilizer, turning it into the ground underneath the orange, tangerine, and lemon trees. Cultivating the ground around the rosebushes and keeping furrows clear so that the wells would water the roses that Bill tenderly gave his wife.

As I looked down on this man that I truly did not come to know, it dawned on me that I had in fact learned something from him. The rose bushes were now no more than thorny sticks in the ground. The beautiful roses had dwindled into history. The oranges, tangerines and lemons no longer produced and the trees stood as aging stumps. Without nurturing, they had withered.

I remember a bit from a poem by Stanley Kunitz, who often writes of gardening and its life metaphors:

_Since that first morning when I crawled
into the world, a naked grubby thing,
and found the world unkind,
my dearest faith has been that this
is but a trial: I shall be changed._

—Stanley Kunitz, _Hornworm, Autumn
Lamentation_

Standing above my emaciated father, curled up tight as sin on his deathbed, I realized that I had changed. I could see him instructing a young boy while they worked in the garden. I learned from him on those Saturday mornings more than how to make a plant grow. I remembered conversations about responsibility, making what you can of what you have. He asked me every time I completed a task: "Was it a good job or a bad job?" I learned how to plant a life and make it grow even when I found the world unkind.

I had been staring out the window for some time when I turned and asked the care giver, "Do you need a break?"

"Yes, I could use a walk."

I heard the front door close as she left and there I stood with my father in the home alone. I moved closer to the bedside and placed my hand lightly on his wrinkled hand. His hand lifted as if to say _don't touch me._ I disregarded the gesture as a reflex and placed my hands gently on his shoulder, held his face, stroked the side of his head before resting my hands on his forehead. He didn't resist, only slowed his breathing.

I whispered: "I love you."

A sense of stillness came over me and I was moved to offer a prayer. As a son, I asked God to forgive this man, to accept the good that he had done. I prayed peace be upon him, and love between us. I closed in the name of the Savior, the Jesus I had come to know as loving, kind, patient, not vindictive or vengeful. I stood for a moment longer, feeling peace in that house for the first time in my life, my father's soft breaths rising and falling, the only sound in the home. I wept for a moment, for all that I missed, and for all that I had gained.

The care giver returned and sat quietly in a chair in my father's room. A half an hour later, while driving to the airport, my older sister called. She said she had just heard from the care giver. Bill had passed quietly and peacefully.

EPILOGUE

Noli Timere
(Don't be afraid)
—*Last words of the Irish poet*
Seamus Heaney

After my uncle's Ben's 1985 death there was the customary reading of the will and settling the estate. His last will and testament was sent to me and there was one particular area that stood out to me for its unabashed irony. In his will he asked that 200 masses be offered for the repose of his soul and paid $1000 for the masses. He asked the society for the propagation of the faith for these masses and that the gift and bequest be satisfied before all other debts. Interesting to note: the Catholic Church outlawed the sale of indulgences in 1567. Still, charitable contributions can help you earn one. I guess in the Monsignor's mind, it was still a viable way to erase any sins, particularly those that may become known after his death. I was neither surprised nor upset by his request, simply amused.

I have pondered this over the years many times and come to the conclusion that the simple words by Gandhi are a definite more appropriate way to live. He said:

"Happiness is when what you think, what you say, and what you do are in harmony."

I have tried to live in harmony with God and let others find their way. Anger absolves nothing. Once away from my oppressive upbringing I was able to read the bible as a kind of self-improvement manual. I found the teachings of Christ to be deep and enduring. I have learned that this life is a time to prepare to meet God, not to prepare justifications for our failings. Why would prayers need to be given at the end of a life as opposed to trying to live a good life? Why live your life in the dark shadows indulging lust, deceit, greed, and power while publicly passing swift judgment with the waive of a gilded arm and the nod of a crowned head? The parish is where broken people come to heal, not a place to become broken. My uncle lived two different lives to satisfy his most prurient desires. I wonder if his antithetical soul will be eternally at war with itself.

As I move on with my life, untangling myself from the Hawkes' web, there remains in me just a bit of fear—fear that was ingrained by both Bill and Ben when I was a child. With each recounting of my story, I cast off the sad history and look to a positive future.

Thank you for reading. I author this story because I want you, the reader, to know that every child deserves to be loved. That there should be no distinction based on how they came into a family. Children are not property or bitter fruit. They are God's cherished gift to all of us and should be treated as such. Additionally, I share this as a cautionary message to those entrusted with the care and safety of children. Sexual predators are masters at hiding their crimes and they often seek out the vulnerable and children in tenuous family situations. They may threaten victims and their families to ensure silence. Be vigilant in protecting children from sexual predators.

As a parting scene I offer two distinct memories after my adoptive father died. The first is coming home to Susan and the kids, wrapping them in my arms and feeling

like the luckiest man on earth.

The second is sardonic and tragic. Bill Hawkes had no service, per his wishes. He was to be buried in the family plot in Los Angeles. The mortuary had one of their employees drive the body down in a van. My older adoptive sister called to tell us she would not be there, nor would be her twin sister. "Could you meet the van at the grave?" "Of course," I answered. It was the second graveside service that the two orphans would attend— the only two of four children that would pay their final respects.

My biological twin sister brought her son. I brought Susan, our son, and dear friends Bob and Clyde. The van pulled up and the driver climbed out. The doors were flung open like a delivery van, and I looked inside to see my father's casket, an ordinary, pressed cardboard box, per his wishes, containing my father's remains. Bob, Clyde, my nephew, my son, the van driver, and I served as pallbearers as together we lifted my father to his final resting place.

I offered a simple prayer.

William Irving Hawkes was buried in the same plot as his wife Helen. Next to him was buried The Right Reverend Monsignor Benjamin Hawkes. Here were the two most prominent men in my early life, two that had caused so much pain, and now lay silent. I put my arm around my wife. I had a life to make meaningful with Susan, our children, and grandchildren.

My sister and I watched as the dirt was shoveled into the hole, two banished Irish babies, now adults. I honestly can't remember if tears were shed that day or not. I suspect that if anybody felt anything it was that we missed out. We missed out on having grandparents for our children, on bonds that grow stronger as they grow older, of simply being loved.

Yes, my life was at times incredibly sad and unfortunate, however; I realized that day that we are not given a good life or a bad life. We are given a life to make good or bad. I had my life ahead of me to make good for my children and my grandchildren.

One day as Susan and I were unpacking our boxes getting ready to move into the home we would retire in, the phone rang. On the other end was a voice of someone I did not know. She explained that we were neighbors and wanted to know if they could come by and introduce themselves and get to know us. "Sure," was my response. We had moved to retire close to our children and weren't anxious to get involved in the neighborhood. I jokingly turned to Susan and said, "close all the blinds, seal up the doors, the neighbors are coming at us, we have been found out"!!!

Soon the doorbell rang, and we opened to look at a couple about our age. We all sat down on the couch and had introductory pleasantries. One of the questions that's always asked is, "Tell us where you're from, where did you go to school, how did you meet." For Susan it's a pretty simple answer. For me to answer the question usually brings us around to the discussion of Ireland. What was going to be a short encounter extended into a long meeting. Near the end of the meeting as the couple were walking out the man turned me and said: "let's get lunch soon I'd like to hear a little bit more of your story it sounds very fascinating."

A week later this fellow named Steve and I met at a local Italian restaurant to grab a cheese and salami sandwich. It was at this meeting where I told him more about my story where I was from, and so on and so forth. He said to me that he was a writer and had authored a few books and was very intrigued with this my story. I told him that we had written a draft of my story but had been looking for the right ghostwriter. I asked if he would be interested in him helping turn the story into a book, a memoir. Then he went on to explain why he found my story compelling. I cannot do his motivations for helping me any justice so I will let Steve deliver it in his words.

I'm not the sort who likes to write other people's stories. I write fiction and that suits me. But when I met Mike, something stirred deep inside that had been rotting in the corners of my soul, something that had to be told. My story is of a lively twelve-year-old boy wanting, like all boys that age, to be part of the tribe—the pack of boys who spend their days on dusty fields with old footballs or cracked-leather baseball gloves in endless chatter, movement, and joy. I had that. I had an idyllic childhood, parents who loved and let consequences be the teacher. Family, especially siblings, who I could share great adventures with, and sometimes take a fist in the nose for. It's this ideal childhood that made my sixth-grade year so hard to reconcile. My teacher sexually molested me. He was a big man, with a big voice that used to rail against communists and favor the fair-skinned boys in his class, then shepherd them to the back of the room and molest them during science movies. This was a

secret I could not unlock for fear of how its torrents
would wash me away from my family forever.
It was, after all, my fault. My shame. Pandora's
box of emotions would remain locked. The next
year, a boy in that man's class did reveal what
was happening. He was teased mercilessly. He
committed suicide. I buried the box.

What I found in authoring this story was an easing
of the weight I carried. A twelve-year-old boy is
not responsible for the actions of a lecherous man. I
was not responsible for the suicide of another. I was
not a disappointment to my family. I was not to be
cast out by God but rather was embraced by Him.
I reflected on the years and years of life I had lived
so close to God's reach, sometimes embracing it, and
sometimes withdrawing. And finally healing.

This book was a journey for me too. It should be a
call to arms to all good people to stand up to those
who would harm our children with such debased
actions. The harm it creates can last generations.
But if we prevent it, and embrace those who
have been afflicted, the love can burst forth like
the waters of Moses. To parents, be vigilant. To
victims, don't be afraid. We are with you.

ACKOWLEDGEMENTS

Virtually no facet of my journey or the authoring of this book could have been accomplished by me alone. The memoir is mine, but the journey, research, and outcomes are shared endeavors.

To my twin sister, who was with me during our early life from before birth, to orphanage, and to our adopted home, where our formative years continued in California; Your love and support have always meant so much to me and I am grateful: I love you.

To our first parents Betty and Patrick, Thank you for getting us safely delivered and then securely to Ireland which set the stage for all that transpired in getting us to America. I love you, 'til we meet again.

To my adopted parents Helen and Bill, I love you and am grateful for your care, support, and good lessons you taught.

To my co-author and wonderful wife, Susan: Words cannot express how grateful I am for you and all the things that we have experienced together the last 40 plus years. From the day I told you of my story of having been adopted from an Irish orphanage, and your reply that Oliver Twist was a favorite of yours, what a joy it has been to have you by my side in life and in completion of this endeavor.

I love you dearly with my whole heart.

To our children, their spouses, and our grandchildren, those here on earth and those we will meet again: I love and appreciate you immensely. You are my joy.

To Susan's Parents, Ken and Sharon Griener: I love you and appreciate the example you set as the extraordinary loving parents and grandparents that you are. Thank you, Sharon, for your final look at our manuscript with an expert eye for all things literary!

To our newfound family, How grateful I am for your courage, love, and acceptance in a delicate situation.

To Tony Beatty: I am so grateful for your initial enthusiastic correspondence with us regarding my mother, your cousin. You met us with even more enthusiasm in Dublin on our first trip to Ireland. It was a profound experience to take a short walk from our hotel to the red door, where you had discovered was the last place my mother said goodbye to her two children. I am so appreciative of continued friendship with you and your family.

To Maura, Eddie, and Catherine who loved my mother and sister and me in the early months: Thank you profoundly. Meeting Maura and hearing the story from a personal witness was one of the treasures of my journey.

To our dear Cleary cousins Rose, Noreen, and Philip; Thank you for your tenacity in finding me Rose! Thank you, Noreen, and Philip, for your extraordinary genealogical research and sharing that treasure with us. I will never forget our first meeting at our hotel in Dublin and hope for many more gatherings! We love you all and so appreciate your continued friendship.

To my cousin Noel Fanning who was the family genealogist who accepted our messages of enquiry regarding my father Patrick: Thank you Noel for having your extensive family tree on Ancestry.com made public and for responding to our sensitive inquiries! Without your acceptance and responses to our messages, our story would have hit a devastating brick wall. Instead, you responded and gave to us the Ryan Family Pot of Gold for which we had been searching! We love you and so appreciate your continued friendship and family search collaboration.

Speaking of that Pot of Gold; To the Ryan family, a wonderful salt of the Earth family in England, Ireland, and Australia; Your acceptance and love have made a profound change in the trajectory of my life. Barney and his wonderful wife Anne and their children Annette, Kevin, and John all could have said" no, and don't ever call me again". Instead, I now have a brother and extended Ryan family, who opened their hearts as well as their home. We are profoundly enriched by counting Barney and Anne, Annette and Dave and family, Kevin and Nicola and family and John and Leanne as family. Included in that pot of gold are Anne's siblings and their descendants—the Doherty's of Donegal. We are overjoyed to call you family as well.

Although we missed meeting my brother Gerry in this life, we have been delighted to meet his children: Susan and Dave and their families and so appreciate their acceptance and friendship. May Manchester United make all your dreams come true, Dave!

To the Dublin Ryans, as we affectionately refer to them—the Children and grandchildren and beyond of my uncle Michael and his wife Jane: Thank you for welcoming us to the Ryan family as well. Thank you, Ciaran and Farida, for hosting a lovey gathering at which we met numerous extended Ryan cousins.

⸺◦∞◦⸺

Members of the Adoption Rights Alliance and Clann Project have, through their selfless work, aided our search and understanding immensely. I am grateful for you all.

I am deeply appreciative for the association with all those we have met on this journey.

Milton Keynes UK
Ingram Content Group UK Ltd.
UKHW010930280823
427620UK00001B/200